Coming to
CHRIST

Coming to
CHRIST

Resting in His Love

Susan Conroy

Our Sunday Visitor Publishing Division
Our Sunday Visitor
Huntington, Indiana 46750

Nihil Obstat
Msgr. Michael Heintz, Ph.D.
Censor Librorum

Imprimatur
✠ Kevin C. Rhoades
Bishop of Fort Wayne-South Bend
August 4, 2014

The *Nihil Obstat* and *Imprimatur* are official declarations that a book is free from doctrinal or moral error. It is not implied that those who have granted the *Nihil Obstat* and *Imprimatur* agree with the contents, opinions, or statements expressed.

Every reasonable effort has been made to determine copyright holders of excerpted materials and to secure permissions as needed. If any copyrighted materials have been inadvertently used in this work without proper credit being given in one form or another, please notify Our Sunday Visitor in writing so that future printings of this work may be corrected accordingly.

ISBN: 978-1-61278-781-7 (Inventory No. T1587)
eISBN: 978-1-61278-358-1
LCCN: 2014942470

Cover design: Amanda Falk
Cover photo: Lisa Elizabeth Photography, Falmouth, Maine
Interior design: Dianne Nelson
Interior photos: See "Photo Credits" (page 125)

PRINTED IN THE UNITED STATES OF AMERICA

In loving memory of Mom and Dad,
who taught us the most beautiful ways
of coming to Christ.

"The people who sit in darkness / have seen a great light, / on those dwelling in a land overshadowed by death / light has arisen" (Matthew 4:16).

❧

This book is unique in that it blossomed from a television series! It is filled with reflections on how to come to our Lord Jesus and find refreshment and peace. It contains the very basics of our faith — which are vital to us all, because to find Jesus Christ is to find salvation, since "no one comes to the Father except through" Jesus (John 14:6).

My father used to say, "Remember God, and He will remember you." Throughout these pages, we will be sharing ways to keep turning to God and returning to God.

This material was first presented and filmed outdoors in the state of Maine, overlooking both the Atlantic Ocean and the mountains. We were surrounded by God's glorious creation — because natural beauty draws us closer to Christ and raises our minds and hearts to Him. Our Lord Jesus liked to be near the sea — and so did the apostles. They also liked to climb mountains to pray to our Heavenly Father. In imitation of Christ, we went to the mountains and to the sea!

❧

Filming the first segment of the
Coming to Christ *series.*

TABLE OF CONTENTS

Practically speaking, how do we draw near to God in this life?
It is important, because that is how we will find lasting peace
and reach our ultimate goal of everlasting life. We start with an
overview of ways that we can come to Christ in response to His
wonderful invitation: **"Come to me, all you who labor and
are burdened, and I will give you rest"** (Matthew 11:28).

Chapter 2:

Saint John Vianney said that "if we really understood the Mass,
we would die of joy." At every Mass, we are able to receive Jesus
Christ Himself in Holy Communion and hear His words of everlasting life. We have the privilege of embracing the very Word
of God. Saint Leonard of Port Maurice exclaimed: **"O blessed
Mass, by which we come to have the Son of God placed
not within our arms, but within our hearts!"**

In adoration of the Most Blessed Sacrament, we *bask* in the light and peace of Christ in the most holy Eucharist. We will speak about prayer and the importance of silence and inner peace. The great Saint Teresa of Ávila said: **"Give me a person who has fifteen minutes of mental prayer daily, and I will give you a saint."**

Our Lord Jesus told Saint Faustina that when we approach the confessional, we should know that He Himself is waiting there for us: "I am only hidden by the priest, but I Myself act in your soul. Here the misery of the soul meets the God of mercy ..." (*Diary*, 1602). As Saint Paul said, **"Let us confidently approach the throne of grace to receive mercy and to find grace for timely help"** (Hebrews 4:16). All that grace and peace is right there waiting for us!

We will share some thoughts on joy — the joy of loving our Lord, and the importance of sharing joy with one another. The world can seem so dark at times, so **"[P]ut your heart into** being a bright light," as Mother Teresa of Calcutta used to say. This is one of the most beautiful fruits of resting in Christ's love and one of the most beautiful ways of *spreading* the light of Christ to others. Our Holy Father, Pope Francis, said that "a life without challenges does not exist," and we will discover that even our sufferings can bring us closer to Christ and thus bring us joy.

Pondering and sharing this material made me love our Savior Jesus even *more*. My hope is that it will do the same for every reader who takes these words to heart.

Setting up for filming the Coming to Christ *series.*

Chapter 1

WHERE DO WE FIND JESUS CHRIST IN OUR LIVES TODAY?

In early June 2013, a group of five cameramen and producers from the Eternal Word Television Network (EWTN) came to my home state of Maine to tape a new television series called *Coming to Christ*. As the name suggests, it is about how to find Jesus. It doesn't get more basic than that — or more *important* than that! Everything I shared was inspired by our Lord's words: **"Come to me, all you who labor and are burdened, and I will give you rest"** (Matthew 11:28). Everything written in these pages is to remind us of how we can come to Christ, so that He can then refresh us and give us rest and peace.

The weather forecast was miserable for the week of EWTN's visit — the kind of forecast that would normally fill hearts with despair at the prospect of taping a television series outdoors. Instead, the week proved to be a journey of faith and a miracle of God's love! It was a most impressive leap of faith on the part of

EWTN! How greatly we all relied on our Lord's mercy to help us bring this project to fruition. The film crew arrived amidst rapidly deteriorating weather conditions, but I prayed, "Jesus and sweet Mother Mary, I know you can do it!"

As Mother Teresa used to say, "Alone we can do nothing — but together, we can do something beautiful for God."

The material I shared in the television presentations could be seen as a follow-up to my earlier series on EWTN, which was called *Speaking of Saints*. Instead of just speaking of saints this time, I was speaking of the KING of all saints, the LORD of all saints, and the perfect MODEL of all saints: Jesus Christ, our Lord and Savior — the love of our life! These two topics actually dovetail together: *Coming to Christ* and *Speaking of Saints*. If we come to Christ, we can *become* saints. One leads to the other, since Jesus is our Redeemer. Saints are always pointing to Jesus Christ, loving Him with all their hearts and souls, and witnessing to Him with their words and with their lives. Jesus and saints go together. He turns sinners *into* saints. It is precisely by finding and following Jesus Christ that we who are sinners can become saints. That is why I am so excited about this topic!

We taped the programs in my beloved state of Maine because natural beauty can draw us closer to Christ — and coming closer to Christ is the whole point! That's the purpose! We were surrounded by the work of God's own hands. There were moments during filming when the sun was shining, the birds were singing, and the sea was sparkling; there were other moments when the sky was overcast, the waves were crashing against the rocky shore, and a cold breeze was blowing. God was being glo-

Filming at Portland Head Light in
Cape Elizabeth, Maine.

rified by it all! He designed the set! Heaven and earth are *full* of His glory! Hosanna in the highest!

What better place to talk about Jesus Christ, the light of the world, than the *lighthouse*-dotted coastline of Maine? Behind me, you can see Portland Head Light, one of the oldest lighthouses in America. The building of this lighthouse was commissioned by President George Washington back in 1790. We could say that our Lord Jesus is the *eternal* beacon of light guiding us through the stormy seas of this life and bringing us safely home to the beautiful and peaceful shores of *everlasting* life. Historically, the Church has been seen as a ship carrying God's children safely to the eternal shores of heaven. The words of Christ and the teachings of Christ's Church are a light to our path. May we always stay in the ship, abiding by the holy faith and morals handed on to us! And may we pray ardently and with great love for those who have "jumped ship" and gone overboard, those who are straying from the beautiful teachings of the Church, especially those who are most dear to us. As my mom and dad often prayed: "Let not one be lost!" That is our battle cry!

Saint Thérèse of Lisieux greatly benefitted from hearing that life is our boat, not our home. We are on a journey. She said that this image gave her peace and strength to put up with the challenges of life's journey through what can sometimes seem like very restless waters. Sometimes people come to me with pains, heartaches, and disappointments — I remind them that we're not in heaven yet. We're still in the valley of tears. We're still on this pilgrimage called "life" which can get pretty rough at times.

We filmed one episode on a grassy peninsula at the end of these rocks, near these little fishermen's shacks overlooking the sea. Our Lord said to Saint Peter that he was "rock," and "upon this rock I will build my church" (Matthew 16:18). May we, too, cherish a rock-solid faith in Jesus Christ!

We have to sail on! Ever onward and upward, as my mom always said! In the end, if we keep the faith and stay with Christ, if we keep following His light and the fullness of truth, we will arrive home in our true fatherland where we can really rest and enjoy unending peace.

Throughout this book, you will see the rocky coastline of Maine. I want it to remind us of the rugged character of our Christian souls as we patiently weather all the challenges of time and tide and tempest. Jesus our head, the master of our ship, brave-ly endured all the sufferings of His life, and He wants us to have courage and inner strength to do the same in our own — weath-ering all our storms with the help of His grace. Sometimes when I'm going through extremely challenging times, I like to recall those words of our Lord, **"My grace is sufficient for you"** (2 Corinthians 12:9). His grace is there for the taking! In abundance!

I also want us to let this beautiful Atlantic Ocean remind us of our Lord's tidal waves of grace, the torrents of His love for us, the infinite expanse of God's goodness, and the ocean of His divine mercy! Our Lord Jesus went and lived by the sea when He began His public ministry of preaching. It was by the sea that the apostles became fishermen ... and fishers of *men*.

Again, this entire book is based on our Lord's words: **"Come to me, all you who labor and are burdened, and I will give you rest"** (Matthew 11:28).

I have to admit that for many years, when I heard this Gospel passage, I wanted to raise my hand and say: "Here I am, Lord! I am weary, I am heavy-burdened, and I am longing for refreshment!" I really identify with that longing for rest, especially as I get older.

As a translator, I can tell you that there are a few slightly varying translations of Matthew 11:28:

- "Come to me, all of you who are tired from carrying heavy loads, and I will give you rest."

- "Come to me, all who labor and are heavy laden, and I will give you rest."

- "Come to me, all you who are weary and find life burdensome, and I will refresh you."

No matter how we translate it, I think we all understand what Jesus is trying to say.

In light of our Lord's promise to refresh us, I again think it's wonderful to get glimpses of the ocean as we talk about coming to Christ. I actually go swimming in these waters, and I can tell you that no matter how hot the air temperature might get in Maine during the summer, the minute you jump into the water here, you are instantly refreshed! Christ's love is like that. When I swim in these waters, I always think of our Lord and how "*in him* we live and move and have our being" (Acts 17:28). Every day, it's like we are swimming in His presence and in His loving kindness. The very fact that we exist and are breathing is a sign of His merciful love for us. He wants us to remain in His love: Swim around in it and find joy in it!

As God's children, we are supposed to seek him — "even perhaps grope for him and find him, though indeed he is not far from any one of us," as Saint Paul says (Acts 17:27). God

*One segment of the series was filmed within view of this
simple sandy beach in Maine. I delight in the fact
that God made that beautiful ocean and those
islands offshore, and that soft sand and the gorgeous
sky and those sweet-smelling, white sea roses.*

made us to seek Him and find Him: "Our hearts are restless until
they rest in Him," as St. Augustine said. To find God is to find
peace. It is like coming HOME. It is like taking off a tight shoe.

Yet I notice that a lot people spend their time, talent, and
treasure seeking everything BUT Christ — seeking *temporary*
things that are far less valuable. People earnestly pursue things
that are worth nothing compared to God and heaven, when,
in the words of Saint Thérèse, "only that which is eternal can
satisfy us." I have a piece of paper taped to my wall at home

with a quotation by Blessed Jacinta of Fátima, one of the little shepherd children who saw our beautiful Blessed Mother Mary. She was shown a vision of hell that set her heart on fire to save souls from the fires of hell. This little child said: "If men only knew what eternity is, they would do everything in their power to change their lives."

A friend of mine from Toronto said it's too bad all of us weren't shown a vision of hell — to keep us on track towards heaven and keep our lives more pleasing to God. His words reminded me of how Father Charles Arminjon shared, in his book *The End of the Present World and the Mysteries of the Future Life,* that Saint Ignatius of Loyola, a former soldier, said that he knew of no sermons more useful and beneficial than those on hell.

- "Reflections on the beauties of virtue and the delights and attractions of divine love have little influence upon coarse, sensual men. Amidst the noisy pleasures of their lives, the seductive bad examples set before them, the traps and pitfalls set beneath their feet, the threat of hell is the only curb powerful enough to keep them on the path of duty."
- "For this same reason, Saint Teresa of Ávila would often bid her austere nuns to go down to hell in spirit and thought during their life, so as to avoid going there in reality after their death."

With everything we do in life, we should be asking ourselves: Where is this behavior leading me ETERNALLY? Is this bringing me closer to God and eternal happiness, or further away? What is at the end of this path that I'm on? And if we're heading in the *wrong* direction, we should redirect our lives, turn the steering wheel.

This is exactly why Father Arminjon wrote his book about the end of the present world — because people were neglecting the most important matters of all: the state of their soul and their future destiny, their unending happiness and rest, which is attained through coming to Christ and following Him all the way. Father Arminjon, way back in the late 1800s, said that "the fatal error and great plague of our century" is "the absence of the sense of the supernatural and the profound neglect of the great truths of the future life." People were *forgetting* about the Day of Judgment and not preparing with care for a happy ending to life's journey. Couldn't we say the same thing about our culture today? Doesn't it sometimes look like a lot of us have our foot on the gas pedal, heading straight towards the cliff of eternal *punishment* and *pain*? It's so important to be faithful and far-sighted in all that we do. Always look ahead to where everything is leading you.

It is of vital importance that we — as individuals, as families, and as a nation — find Jesus, come to know Him, and be *close* to Him. It has *eternal* consequences. It's literally a matter of life and death. ETERNAL life and death.

❧

There is an entire chapter in Father Arminjon's book on heaven. It is titled "Eternal Beatitude and the Supernatural Vision of God." This is the chapter that enormously inspired Saint Thérèse of Lisieux and gave her a foretaste of the happiness of heaven while she was still on earth. It taught her that God Himself will be our "great and eternal reward" if we strive to stay in the light and keep to His loving ways. The more we realize what *awaits* us in heaven, and WHO awaits us in heaven with such love and longing, the more joy and peace we will have in *this* life. The more we realize the eternal rewards and blessings that are to come, and *direct our lives accordingly,* the more our life on *earth* will be hope-filled and holy. We will also have more courage to endure whatever trials and tribulations come our way, knowing that "heaven will make up for everything."

Saint Francis de Sales tells us that we should live in this life as if we already had one foot in the door of heaven! His exact words were that: "We should live in this world as though our *spirits* were already in heaven." I love that. As we continuously come to Christ and keep our eyes fixed on our Lord, we can live lives on earth full of peace.

- Full of joyful hope.

- Full of the most pure and ardent love for God and for one another.

- Full of God's own goodness, as true children of God.

- Full of the power of confidence in our Heavenly Father, knowing that "confidence in God works miracles" (Saint Thérèse).

*A gentle sunset at the beach where we taped
our third episode of* Coming to Christ.

- Full of praise and adoration and endless thanksgiving to God.

"It is right to give him thanks and praise," as we used to say at Mass. It is "our duty and our salvation," and "we do well always and everywhere to give [him] thanks."

I think that if we can learn to come to Christ and *immerse ourselves* in God's love here and now — just as I immerse myself in that glorious Atlantic Ocean and find instant refreshment — then we will *rest* in God's love and find refreshment for all eternity. We begin our heaven *now*. And closeness to Jesus is heaven.

Saint Catherine of Siena said, "All the way to heaven is heaven because of Him Who is the way." The realization of Who is by our side throughout life's journey turns our darkness into light and our mourning into joy — even if we are suffering.

Many years ago, I was at a point in my own personal journey where everything seemed like misery and I couldn't see any light at the end of the tunnel. A holy Carmelite priest wrote to me that if you can't see any light at the end of the tunnel, just remember that Jesus is in the tunnel too. That changed everything! The Lord is with us. What a comforting truth to hold on to! We have every reason to keep smiling. We have hope because we have Christ.

Pope Emeritus Benedict XVI wrote that "we go to heaven to the extent that we go to Jesus Christ and enter into him," and he also said, "Jesus himself is what we call 'heaven.'"

꙰

Jesus says, "Come to me," and this is the whole purpose of our life. The purpose of our existence is to come to God — come to know, love, and serve the Lord our God so that we can be reasonably happy in *this* life and *supremely* happy with Him in everlasting life. We exist for the praise of His glory — and being united with Christ Jesus is our destiny. Sharing His eternal happiness is our inheritance: It is the glorious inheritance of the saints.

Now the million-dollar question: What does it *mean* to "come" to our Lord Jesus? How do we actually do that? I am a very practical person, and I always want to know *how* to practice our faith, *how* to come close to God, and *how* to reach our goal. What are the actual steps to take? It's so important for us to know how to come to Christ and where to find Him. This is the real "meat and potatoes" of our faith!

I started thinking about some of the big ways of finding Jesus Christ in this life, and in this first chapter, I want to give a brief summary of them:

1. We come to our Lord Jesus at *Holy Mass.*

This is the biggest and most powerful way of all. Saint John Vianney used to point to the tabernacle and say: "He is there! Jesus is there!"

Jesus Himself "took bread, said the blessing, broke it, and giving it to his disciples said, 'Take and eat; this is my body.' Then he took a cup, gave thanks, and gave it to them, saying,

'Drink from it, all of you, for this is my blood of the covenant, which will be shed on behalf of many for the forgiveness of sins' " (Matthew 26:26-28). We come to Jesus Christ in a very real way in Holy Communion. With pure faith in *His own* words, we share in this holy union with our Lord! We can't get any closer to Christ in this life than by taking Him to heart in Holy Communion, and letting His own Precious Blood literally flow through our veins.

Pope Francis emphasizes the importance of celebrating Mass: "Dear friends, we don't ever thank the Lord enough for the gift he has given us in the Eucharist! It is a very great gift and that is why it is so important to go to Mass on Sunday. Go to Mass not just to pray, but to receive Communion, the bread that is the body of Jesus Christ who saves us, forgives us, unites us to the Father. It is a beautiful thing to do!" He also said, "The Eucharist is the summit of God's saving action: The Lord Jesus, by becoming bread broken for us, pours upon us all of his mercy and his love, so as to renew our hearts, our lives and our way of relating with him and with the brethren" (General Audience, February 5, 2014).

We will do a whole chapter on this most beautiful, powerful, and effective way of coming to Jesus Christ! To reiterate, the number-one way we come to Jesus is in the Mass, in Holy Communion with Christ, Who commanded us to **"do this in memory of me"** (Luke 22:19).

Now let's continue with our overview of various ways to come to Him.

2. We come to our Lord Jesus in *Confession*.

When I partake in the Sacrament of Reconciliation — longing to know clearly and fulfill faithfully *God's* will for my life — I love to recall what our Lord Jesus said to Saint Faustina: "Be obedient to your director in everything; his word is My Will. Be certain in the depths of your soul that it is I Who am speaking through his lips, and I desire that you reveal the state of your soul to him with the same simplicity and candor as you have with Me. I say it again, My daughter: know that his word is My Will for you" (*Diary*, 979). How carefully I listen to the spiritual counsel that is given to me in the confessional! How earnestly I want to abide by it, cost what it may, with the help of God's grace!

Through the Sacrament of Penance, we are reconciled to God and to others. As Pope Francis reminds us: "Too often, we see ourselves as the center and measure of all things, and our lives can go adrift. The Sacrament of Reconciliation calls us back to God, and embraces us with his infinite mercy and joy. May we allow his love to renew us as his children and to reconcile us with him, with ourselves, and with one another" (General Audience, February 19, 2014).

3. We come to our Lord Jesus at *Adoration*.

How blessed we are to be able to "make a visit" with our Lord in the Most Holy Sacrament. He is always there waiting for us, He Who loves us so much. When His Divine Majesty is hidden in the tabernacle, it is still an unspeakable honor to be near Him. When He is exposed in the Most Blessed Sacrament, that is an even greater joy. One day, when He comes to take us home, He will pull aside the veil of that sweet encounter and we will see Him face-to-face. That will be the greatest joy of all! Just the *thought* of it fills my eyes with tears. We begin our heaven on earth. In communion with the saints, we lovingly adore our Savior here and now, as we will adore Him forever. Let us ask for the grace to love Him as purely and ardently as the saints do in heaven.

Advocating the practice of Eucharistic Adoration, Pope Francis said: "The first thing for a disciple is to be with the master, to listen to him and to learn from him....It means abiding in the Lord's presence and letting ourselves be led by him." He went on to say, "Do you let yourselves be gazed upon by the Lord? But how do you do this? You look at the tabernacle and you let yourselves be looked at ... it is simple!" What if you fall asleep? "Fall asleep then, sleep! He is still looking at you." He said that being in our Lord's presence and letting Him look at us "is itself a way of praying" (Address to Catechists, September 27, 2013).

He truly sees you, he is close to you, and he loves you. Pope Francis asks: "Do I find time to remain in his presence, in silence, to be looked upon by him? Do I let his fire warm my heart? If the warmth of God, of his love, of his tenderness is not in our own hearts, then how can we, who are poor sinners, warm the heart of others?" (Address to Catechists, September 27, 2013).

4. We come to our Lord Jesus when we *gather in His Name.*

When we come together as a prayer group, at a holy book study, as a family when we pray together, and especially at Mass, we come to our Lord Jesus. He assured us that where two or more are gathered in His Name, He will be in our midst: I have always found that so consoling and refreshing! The Lord wants us to "be brought to perfection as one" (John 17:23). He wants us to come together in His Holy Name.

Pope Francis talks about *starting anew with Christ* and how that means "being close to him, being close to Jesus." He said that "Jesus uses the image of the vine and the branches and says: Abide in my love, remain attached to me, as the branch is attached to the vine. If we are joined to him, then we are able to bear fruit. This is what it means to be close to Christ. Abide in Jesus! This means remaining attached to him, in him, talking to him. Abide in Jesus" (Address to Catechists, September 27, 2013).

5. We come to our Lord Jesus in *His Living Word.*

Jesus is the Word made flesh! Scripture says: "In the beginning was the Word, / and the Word was with God, / and the Word was God.... And the Word became flesh / and made his dwelling among us" (John 1:1, 14). And His Name is Jesus. I actually kiss my holy Bible and press it to my heart, because this is the word of God — God's holy and eternal word! If you look closely at some of these photographs, you can see that I even held the word of God throughout the taping of each episode of this series *Coming to Christ*.

In the New Testament of our family Bible, the words attributed to Jesus Christ appear in red print: They stand out from all the others (which are in black print), inspiring us to pay extra-close attention to every word that comes from the mouth of God. This is the Lord our GOD speaking! His word is *living* and *effective*. For example, when God said, **"Let there be light"** (Genesis 1:3), there *was* light. And when Jesus said, **"Be still!"** the waters and winds obeyed His word and were calmed and quieted (Mark 4:39). That is why we say to Him: "Only say the word and my soul shall be healed." We trust in His word. We revere the power of His word. We turn to Him and *re*-turn to Him in His living word, living and active. I find that reading the word of God is also like visiting with Him — right in our own living room.

When my beloved dad was dying, I would ask if he wanted me to read to him and he always said yes. I would read him the Holy Gospels at night — and it was like our Lord Jesus was right there in the room *with* us. We could feel His presence as we read His holy word together. Saint Augustine pointed out that when we pray, we speak to God — but when we read Sacred Scripture, God speaks to us. That communication leads to a *closer relationship with our Lord*. Saints are *friends* with God. We all have a chance to draw near to Him and get to know Him more intimately by paying attention to the words that came from His own sacred lips and His own Sacred Heart. What's more, Jesus said clearly: "Whoever loves me will keep my word, and my Father will love him, and we will come to him and make our dwelling with him" (John 14:23). God comes to us and lives with us when we keep His word, when we cherish and obey His holy word. He said so.

6. We come to our Lord Jesus *in our hearts.*

We invite Jesus into our hearts through *prayer,* always and everywhere, even in our sufferings and daily labors. Did you know that Saint Thérèse sometimes felt God's inspirations more when she was on her feet working than when she was on her knees praying? I sometimes find that too — a comforting awareness of God's presence even while doing dishes or watering the lawn; God is close to us in our everyday living. The kingdom of God is within us. Another name for Jesus is "Emmanuel," which means **"God with us."** He is with us.

7. We come to our Lord Jesus *with and through our Blessed Mother Mary.*

This is, in my opinion, one of the sweetest ways to come to Christ. She is His mom and she knows exactly where to find Him. In Holy Scripture, the angel of the Lord appears to Mary and says: **"The Lord is with you"** (Luke 1:28). That is a timeless statement. The Lord is always with Mary and she is always with the Lord. She was actually one with Him: For nine months, He was completely hidden within her and totally dependent on her. Who else can say that? She is *perpetually* the **"handmaid of the Lord"** (Luke 1:38).

Even now, she lives to serve Him. Her role is to bring Jesus to us, and to bring us to Jesus. That is her whole purpose — to help save our souls. When we meditate on the sacred mysteries of our faith while praying the Rosary, it is like sitting on a sofa with our Blessed Mother Mary and flipping through the pages of a photo album of Christ's life. No one knew His life more intimately than she did, because she was there through it all, from the cave in Bethlehem to the cross in Jerusalem. No one else in all of human history can say that. No one but she and Saint Joseph saw what happened in the private life of Christ during all those many hidden years in their own home in Nazareth.

We should be praying more Rosaries! *Many* more! Because praying the Holy Rosary binds us to the Immaculate Heart of Mary. It is the *sure means* of having her always close to us. When we come close to Our Lady, we come close to Christ. The angel of the Lord said so: **"Hail, favored one! The Lord is with you"** (Luke 1:28).

8. We come to our Lord Jesus *when we die.*

In actuality, He comes to us. He comes and takes us to Himself and gives us rest as He promised. We can bet our life on His wonderful promises, and we can take Him at His word — because He is faithful and true. He told us that in His Father's house there are many dwelling places and that He is going to prepare a place for us (John 14:2).

I can't tell you how much I cherish those words. I trust in those words. They are so comforting, and they are true. Our Lord Jesus then said, "I will come back again and take you to myself, so that where I am you also may be" (John 14:3). How I have longed for this since my childhood! When Jesus comes to take me home, I am going to smile at Him and say, "O Lord, what took You so long! I have waited and waited!" I anticipate and hope with all my heart that my last breath will be the happiest moment of my life because of what comes next and Whose face I'll see.

9. We come to our Lord Jesus *through loving and serving one another.*

This is a powerful and meaningful way that we can come to our Lord, especially when we serve those who are most in need of mercy. Jesus said, "[W]hatever you did for one of these least brothers of mine, you did for me" (Matthew 25:40). Whenever we reach out to anyone who is suffering, lonely, sick, poor, or in prison, we reach out to Jesus Christ. He said so. As Mother Teresa said, "We have it in our power to be happy with God at this very moment" — to come very close to Christ by loving and caring for Him "in His distressing disguise of the poor." Mother Teresa also said that "God has created us for great

things: to LOVE and to OFFER LOVE, to experience TEN-
DERNESS towards others, just as He did, and to know how to
offer JESUS to others."

I cannot go into all nine of these ways of coming to Christ
in depth, but I am going to touch briefly on a few of them
throughout this book. And our first way of coming to Jesus is the
most awesome of all — and that is in the Mass. We will dedicate
our entire next chapter to it!

I would like to conclude this first chapter with these comforting words of Psalm 23, which tie in beautifully with what
this *entire* book is about, because when we come to Christ, He
leads us beside waters of peace to our Father's house, where only
goodness and kindness will follow us:

The LORD is my shepherd;
    there is nothing I lack.
In green pastures he makes me lie down;
    to still waters he leads me;
    he restores my soul.
He guides me along right paths
    for the sake of his name.
Even though I walk through the valley of the
        shadow of death,
    I will fear no evil, for you are with me;
    your rod and your staff comfort me.

You set a table before me
    in front of my enemies;

You anoint my head with oil;
    my cup overflows.
Indeed, goodness and mercy will pursue me
    all the days of my life;
I will dwell in the house of the LORD
    for endless days. (Psalm 23:1-6)

The brilliant morning sun rising over the horizon at Portland Head Light in Maine, where we filmed the first episode of Coming to Christ.

We taped the second episode of Coming to Christ *at the refreshing Atlantic Ocean in my beloved home state of Maine.*

Chapter 2

COMING TO CHRIST
AT HOLY MASS

Our Lord gave us a wonderful invitation: "Come to me, all you who labor and are burdened, and I will give you rest" (Matthew 11:28). In response to that invitation, we are going to delve into ways that we can come to Christ and rest in His love. This is such an important topic because in finding Jesus Christ, we find salvation. Jesus is our hope. Jesus is our peace. He is our truth, our love, our everything. As a matter of fact, even the *greatest* saint of modern times, Saint Thérèse of Lisieux, admitted that to reach the ultimate goal of everlasting life, she needed Jesus. We all do. We can't attain holiness, and be saved, and ascend to heaven all by ourselves or by our own power. Saint Thérèse said: "I don't count on my own merits, since I have none — but I trust in Him Who is virtue and holiness." She believed that our Lord alone, content with our weak human efforts to come to Him, will raise us to Himself and clothe us in His own infinite merits.

In our first chapter, I outlined at least nine ways that we can come to Christ. Our Lord promised us that if we who are weary just come to Him, He will refresh us!

Natural beauty raises our minds and hearts to God. I've always felt that the qualities of the ocean in particular have a lot in common with God and His love for us — the unfathomable depth and beauty and infinite expanse. You can't even see the end of it! When St. Thérèse saw the ocean for the first time, it immediately made her think of God. She said, "Never will I forget the impression the sea made upon me; I couldn't take my eyes off it since its majesty, the roaring of its waves, everything spoke to my soul of God's grandeur and power."

While giving you these glimpses of God's greatness and power, I want to focus on our *first* way of coming to Jesus Christ which is the most powerful, awesome, and life-giving of all: the holy and perfect sacrifice of the Mass, the sweet Sacrament of His love.

Our Lord Jesus has so much to give us at every single Mass! Nothing less than Himself! As Saint Thérèse said: "*To love is to give all — and to give oneself.*" That is exactly what Jesus does at every Mass: He gives Himself completely to us! He doesn't hold anything back. At *every* Mass we are able to draw near to Christ not only by listening to His eternal word but also by actually receiving Him in the most Holy Eucharist. Take *hold* of that power of love and those tidal waves of grace. Receive the Body and Blood of Christ with faith. Receive Him with love. Receive Him with reverence. Above all, receive Him with endless thanksgiving and praise. We can't imagine how *blessed* we are to be able to embrace Jesus Christ in the flesh like that —

the Son of the living God! We are allowed to come to the altar and experience this holy union with Christ — so *intimate* that upon receiving Holy Communion, "the adorable Blood of Jesus Christ really flows in our veins and His Flesh is really blended with ours" (St. John Vianney).

Over two thousand years ago, the Blessed Virgin Mary held our Lord Jesus in her arms. In Holy Communion, we hold the *very same* Body, Blood, Soul, and Divinity of Jesus Christ! This is the *greatest privilege* of our life — to hold God like this!

Saint Leonard of Port Maurice said, "O blessed Mass, by which we come to have the Son of God placed not within our arms, but within our hearts!" As my father pointed out to us repeatedly, if we even *half*-realized what takes place during Holy Communion, we would want to crawl to the altar on our knees, knowing that we are not even *close* to being worthy of receiving such a holy and precious gift as the Son of God Most High! How *rightly* we say: "Lord, I am not *worthy* that you should enter under my roof" (emphasis added).

St. John Vianney went so far as to say that "if we really understood the Mass, we would die of JOY."

Frequenting Holy Mass is a way for us to come physically to Christ and then to walk humbly with Him each day, refreshed and strengthened by His real presence within us. When we come and eat His Sacred Flesh and drink His Precious Blood, *as He told us to do*, we have LIFE within us! The everlasting kind of life!

Saint Faustina wrote in her diary: "Every morning ... I prepare myself for the whole day's struggle. Holy Communion assures me that I will *win* the victory; and so it is. I fear the day when I do not receive Holy Communion. This Bread of the Strong gives me all the strength I need to carry on my mission and the courage to do whatever the Lord asks of me. The courage and strength that are in me are not of me, but of Him Who lives in me — it is the Eucharist" (*Diary*, 91). She said: "I do not lose the presence of God in my soul, and I am closely united with Him. With Him I go to work, with Him I go for recreation, with Him I suffer, with Him I rejoice; I live in Him, and He in me. I am never alone, because He is my constant companion" (*Diary*, 318). Jesus told Saint Faustina that He actually delights in coming to us and uniting Himself to our souls. I personally find that *amazing*! It is understandable for us to delight in coming to Christ, since He is God almighty, our wonderful Lord and Savior! But for Him to delight in coming to little nothings like *us*, little *sinful* nothings I might add — that is really remarkable to me.

Jesus said that He actually waits for us, wanting us to unite ourselves with Him in the Most Blessed Sacrament. He told Saint Faustina that He loves us tenderly and sincerely, and wants to "lavish His graces" upon us (*Diary*, 1485). Always remember that in Holy Communion, His hands are full of blessings that He wants to give to us. That's what God does: He gives and gives and gives. That's what love does.

Our Lord also said to Faustina:

Take as many treasures from My Heart as you can carry, for then you will please Me more. And I will tell you one more thing — take these graces not only for yourself, but also for others; that is, encourage the souls

One of the set of lighthouses at Two Lights State Park in Cape Elizabeth, Maine.

with whom you come in contact to trust in My infinite mercy. Oh how I love those souls who have complete confidence in Me — I will do everything for them. (*Diary*, 294)

My personal wish is that all of us will come away from this book with an enormous trust in our Lord's goodness. Jesus said: "Most dear to Me is the soul that strongly believes in My goodness and has complete trust in Me." He said: "I heap My confidence upon it and give it all it asks" (*Diary*, 453).

The Holy Sacrifice of the Mass, like all of the Sacraments of the Church, was instituted by Jesus Christ Himself *to give grace*

— to fill us with His own divine life. To fill us with His own sacred presence. To allow us to come so close to Him as to be one with Him.

Our Lord said: "I want to give Myself to souls and to fill them with My Love ..." (*Diary*, 1017). He basically is saying that He wants to make us saints, because a saint is someone who is filled with the fullness of God, someone in whom Christ lives, someone whose heart is burning with the love of God, with divine love. This is exactly what our Lord wants to give to us during each Holy Communion. I honestly don't think that we half-appreciate how precious is this supreme love-gift: Jesus-the-Eucharist, Divine Love and Divine Life pouring into us each time we come to Him in this *Most* Holy Sacrament.

I keep mentioning how much we receive from Christ at Mass, which is nothing less than His Divine Majesty, but I think it is also vital to remember that after the birth of Jesus, the three Wise Men did not come to Bethlehem seeking the newborn King of the Jews for what they could *get* from Him. They came for what they could *give* to Jesus. They brought their finest gifts to give the King of kings. Like those who are wise, we should come to Mass each week with a longing to give to our Lord Jesus the very best we have — our most sincere worship, our heartfelt thanksgiving, and our most tender love — even though Jesus will never be outdone in generosity and He will lavish us with *far* more than we are even *able* to give Him. But know that we are at Mass to *give* to God, not just to receive from Him. Although this is a simplification, it

Filming this episode on the Holy Mass was done in view of these two lighthouses overlooking the enormous expanse of open ocean.

seems that there are two kinds of people in this world: givers
and takers. Be the givers! Be like Jesus, Who gave *everything He
had*, even His very *life* for us.

A priest once encouraged Saint Thérèse of Lisieux to strive
to "return love for love!" Be His little rival in love. Try to be His
little match (as in a tennis match). As Jesus loves you and lavishes
you with graces, you try to love Him back. You will always be
lovingly conquered! You will never be able to love Him as much
and as dearly as He loves you. But try! Make it a holy competi-
tion between you and our Lord! Let us put our whole hearts
into loving our dear Lord. Let everything in us *rush* towards
loving God.

As we seek to find Christ in our lives, let us look to the Holy
Gospels. When our Blessed Mother Mary and Saint Joseph lost
Jesus and were anxiously searching for Him, where did they find
Him? They found Him in the temple — and this is one of the
places we go to find Jesus. Our Lord said to His holy parents:
"Did you not know that I must be in my Father's house?" (Luke
2:49).

My own dad, as the spiritual leader of our family, always
taught us as children to bless ourselves whenever we drove past
a Catholic church because that is "*God's house*." Our *Lord* lives
there. This is His holy dwelling place on earth where we visit
our Lord and show signs of respect even as we pass by the *outside*
of His house. Jesus is truly present in the Most Holy Sacrament,
and we can come to Him in our Father's house as often as we
want and we will always find Him there.

Our Lord Jesus confirmed this when He said to Saint Faustina: "My Heart overflows with great mercy for souls, and especially for poor sinners. If only they could understand that I am the best of Fathers to them and that it is for them that the Blood and Water flowed from My Heart as from a fount overflowing with mercy. For them I dwell in the tabernacle as King of Mercy. I desire to bestow My graces upon souls.... Come to Me as often as possible," Jesus said, "and take these graces.... In this way, you will console My Heart.... Come to Me for graces," He repeated (*Diary*, 367).

God Himself tells us clearly where to find Him! He said: I dwell in the tabernacle (cf. Revelation 21:3). He has so much love and grace pent up in His Sacred Heart to pour out upon us. He is saying: Come! Take these graces! As *often* as possible! We actually comfort His merciful Heart the more we come and take all His wonderful gifts and blessings.

The older generations like my father and grandfather were faith-filled enough to go and "make a visit" at church to be with Jesus and talk with Him often. My grampa used to stop at the Catholic church every evening on his way home from work and kneel alone in the back pew to make a visit with Jesus. That generation knew Whose presence they were in and what a sacred privilege it was to be near Him. This was part of their daily routine to spend time with our Lord hidden in the Blessed Sacrament.

This reminds me of how the children of Fátima cherished their time with "the hidden Jesus," as they called Him. Blessed little Francisco spent quite a bit of time huddled close to the

As we taped this second episode, I could see this lighthouse before me and the open Atlantic Ocean right beside me. I was sitting on the rugged rocks along the shore.

tabernacle praying the Rosary. When the Angel of Peace — the Guardian Angel of Portugal — first appeared to these little children (before Our Lady started appearing to them), the angel taught them to *prostrate* themselves on the ground before our Eucharistic Lord and to say this prayer: "O Most Holy Trinity — Father, Son and Holy Spirit — I adore Thee profoundly...."

When we step into a Catholic church, we, too, are standing on sacred ground before our Eucharistic Lord, just like the children of Fátima. We would do well to conduct ourselves in like manner when we are in the presence of our Lord Most High. What really *strikes* me in Sacred Scripture — what really *jumps out* at me from the pages of the New Testament — is how, over and over again, when our Lord Jesus Christ was walking the face of the earth over two thousand years ago and people could see His Face (the Holy Face of the Son of God!), they would approach Jesus, fall at His feet, do Him homage, and then beg for favors and blessings. One after another would come to Christ and fall all the way to the *ground* before Him — even rich and very important people who were highly respected in the community. For example:

- The synagogue official named Jairus who came forward and seeing Jesus "*fell at his feet* and pleaded earnestly with him" to save his sick daughter who was at the point of death (Mark 5:22-23).

- The rich young man who threw aside his own dignified manner of moving about and "ran up" to Jesus like an excited little *boy*, and "*knelt down* before him, and asked him, 'Good teacher, what must I do to inherit eternal life?' " (Mark 10:17).

• The woman who had been hemorrhaging for 12 years who "*fell down before Jesus* and told him the whole truth" (Mark 5:33).

• The Greek woman (whose daughter had an unclean spirit) who came "and *fell at his feet* ... [and] begged him to drive the demon out of her daughter" (Mark 7:25, 26).

• The leper who came to Jesus "[and *kneeling down*] begged him and said, 'If you wish, you can make me clean' " (Mark 1:40).

One after the other, they were all coming to Christ and falling at His feet. That position of kneeling on the ground and bowing is a gesture of worship and adoration. We don't do that for one another — we do that only in the presence of God Most High.

It seems to me that, like the *early* Christians, we should be falling at His feet with the same kind of respect as those who beheld His holy Face. We should be approaching Him with far more reverence than we presently manifest when we are in His house each week. It seems that we have become a little nonchalant and almost oblivious of the fact that we are in God's presence. Some of our churches have become a bit like social halls instead of sacred places of worship and adoration. God's house is to be a house of prayer, He said.

Looking at Scripture again, I think it's comforting and instructive to note, too, that Jesus healed, saved, and helped every single person who approached Him with faith — all who came and prostrated themselves before Him and pleaded for His mercy and divine assistance. Jesus helped ALL of them. I never heard of a single time when our Lord sent a sick and suffering person away unhealed and uncared for.

When the leper said, "If you wish, you can make me clean," our Lord Jesus, whose Heart is full of gentleness and compassion, replied, **"I do will it. Be made clean"** (Mark 1:40,41). Jesus wants to heal us. He is almighty; He can do it. He *wants* us all to be well. But He also wants us to meet Him *halfway* with our faith. He repeatedly said: **"Your faith has saved you"** (Luke 7:50; Mark 10:52). **"Everything is possible to one who has faith"** (Mark 9:23). Remember, too, that when He was in His own hometown of Nazareth, He worked very few miracles there because of their lack of faith. We must come to Christ with strong faith. Our part is to trust and believe, and to realize that we are in the presence of an AWESOME God!

After the Lord's resurrection from the dead, Mary Magdalene and the other Mary went away quickly from the empty tomb to announce the good news to His disciples. Scripture says, "Jesus met them on their way and greeted them." What did the women do when they came to Christ? "They approached, embraced his feet, and did him homage" (Matthew 28:9). Think about that. They were hugging His FEET. This is the risen Lord our GOD in front of them! And it is the *same* risen Lord that we have with us now.

This is exactly how we should be conducting ourselves in the presence of our Lord Jesus. We need to rekindle and *recover* that kind of profound reverence, respect, and love for the Holy One. We need to know our place before almighty God. No wonder Saint Teresa of Ávila told us to "kiss His feet in gratitude" after receiving Jesus in Holy Communion! Saint Thomas the Apostle looked at our risen Lord and said, **"My Lord and my God!"** (John 20:28). Each one who encountered Christ was overcome with adoration and AWE. That is why we are taught to say those same exact words when the Body of Christ is held up at the time of consecration: "My Lord and my God!"

I love when Church historian Father Charles Connor celebrates Mass on EWTN, because He elevates the Sacred Host for such an *extended* period of time that it gives us all a chance to say *so much* to our risen Lord: "I love You, Jesus! Thank You, Jesus! I adore You, Lord Jesus!" He really gives us time to express our gratitude, affection, worship, and supplication. This is such a beautiful opportunity to talk with Him and adore Him before we actually approach Him and embrace Him.

The Catholic spiritual classic *The Imitation of Christ* says that we should prepare ourselves with great love and care to receive Christ in Holy Communion. We are like beggars invited to a rich man's supper. Even our best efforts cannot make us worthily prepared for Him — even if we were to prepare for a whole year and do *nothing else* besides! It is because of His mercy and grace *alone* that we are allowed to approach His sacred feast — not because of our own merits. We can offer no return for His kindness except humble gratitude, faithful love, and adoration. We should do everything in our power to receive the precious Body and Blood of our risen Lord Jesus as *worthily* as we can at each Mass, and do it earnestly, with awe and reverent love.

My dad had a wonderful way of approaching Jesus at Mass. He said: "We should take the Blessed Mother's hand on the way to receive Holy Communion. Only for the Blessed Mother, or we'd never make it." Dad so *trusted* in Our Lady's loving care and assistance, and he *marveled* at how "our Blessed Mother *knew* (that her Son was the Holy One)." He said: "Can you imagine *bringing up God!*" He knew that Our Lady is the best one to accompany us to the altar to receive the Body of Christ — because no one received Him more tenderly, adoringly, and *worthily* than His own mom. She can help us to hold Him in our hearts as beautifully as she held Him in her arms. She is the perfect model of receiving Jesus in a most holy way — most pleasing to our Heavenly Father. So, every day now, on my way to the altar, I take Our Lady's hand, just like my dad taught me to do. I believe that Jesus must look at us *with His mother by our side* and smile and say: "You keep good company!"

৵

I would like to share with you another of the *many* incredible blessings of coming to Christ at Holy Mass. Our Lord revealed to Saint Gertrude the Great that "for each Mass we hear with devotion, our Lord sends a saint to comfort us at death." For those of us who are a little bit alone in this life, this is a huge consolation. As someone who is single, without a spouse, without parents, and without children, it really comforts me to know that I won't be all alone at my last breath, even if I *appear* to be alone. If we come to Jesus and devoutly attend Mass, at our last breath we will be surrounded by a whole *entourage* of saints.

Once in a while you hear someone say that they "get nothing" out of Mass. All I can say is: Oh, yes you *do!* You get *far* more than you realize.

One time, when Saint Teresa of Ávila was overwhelmed with God's goodness, she asked our Lord, "How can I thank You?" Our Lord replied: "ATTEND ONE MASS." That's how much it *means* to Him.

So let us COME to Christ with faith at Holy Mass, and come with love, and He will refresh us and make us well.

As I depart from the chapel after Mass each day, I like to say to our Lord: "I am not leaving You; I am bringing You *with* me." I take our Lord with me into the world. *Blessed be God forever* for letting us be so near to Him as to be one with Him and to accompany Him on our way, just like the early Christians did, walking with Christ.

In their retirement years, my mom and dad used to attend daily Mass and Rosary together. As they were nearing the end of their lives, *each* of them earnestly wished to receive our Lord again, and they expressed this wish to us children. We were eager to serve them in every way we could — and my older brothers even offered to *carry* them to Mass if that's what it took. When my brothers led my parents to the altar to receive Jesus, a son on each side holding each of their arms, people would actually *cry* seeing Mom and Dad in such frail condition, barely able to *walk*, still coming to Christ … still coming to Christ.

The morning sun rising over the open Atlantic Ocean at Two Lights State Park in Maine. This was our view as we filmed this second episode of Coming to Christ.

"Two Lights" got its name because of the two lighthouses in close proximity to each other, which is very rare to see. I like to think that these two beacons represent my mom and dad, who were so filled with the light of Christ, guiding us safely home to the beautiful shores of heaven. They handed on to us, their children, "the luminous torch of faith" (Saint Thérèse) and the great light of love. Faith and love are meant to be shared — they are meant to shine forth — to light up everyone's lives! As a matter of fact, before losing my beloved dad, I asked for his blessing, and he put his hands on my head and said: "You have all my blessing and all my love." And then he said something that I would like to hand on to you. He said: "Keep the faith — and help everybody *else* keep the faith."

So, in loving memory of my dear parents, I would like to conclude this chapter with a very old prayer that I actually learned from my dad — who taught me everything I know about coming to Christ:

Dad started this prayer by saying, "Dear Lord Jesus …":

Blood of Christ, fill all my veins.
Water from Christ's side, wash all my stains.
Body of Christ, my comfort be.
O good Jesus, listen to me!
Guard me when the foe assails me.
Call me when my life shall fail me.
Bid me come to Thee above
With Thy saints to *sing Thy LOVE*.
World without end. Amen.

May we sing God's love even here on earth, so that we will sing His love with the saints for all eternity.

Filming at sunrise on the beautiful coast of Maine,
along the Atlantic Ocean.

⨭

Chapter 3

ADORATION AND PRAYER

One summer I had the delightful adventure of kayaking in the Atlantic Ocean along the quiet coast of Maine to a little island offshore, and as I paddled along, there were little seals poking their heads out of the water around me. When I got to the island itself, there were lots of sand dollars, seashells, and beautiful things to discover — even deer and sheep. It was such a fun adventure!

I feel that our Catholic Church is a lot like that treasure-filled place, or like a huge *treasure chest* filled to overflowing with the most exquisite "gems" of graces and blessings, which we can find in abundance. You can reach *into* the Church and pull out all the spiritual "sapphires," "rubies," "diamonds," and "pearls" that your hands can hold or that your heart can carry! And you can keep coming back for MORE! God has an inexhaustible supply of wisdom, graces, and gifts for us in the Catholic Church. As I love to point out, it's all FREE! No limit is set on how much we may gather. For example, in the Church:

- We have *unfathomable* riches and blessings flowing from all the holy Sacraments — each of which is an encounter with Christ.

- We have our Blessed Mother Mary, whose hands are streaming with graces for us.

- We have our brothers and sisters in heaven, called the saints, who are always there to help us — and there are a *lot* of them.

- We have the opportunity to love and serve Jesus in His distressing disguise of the poor — and they too are considered the treasure of the Catholic Church.

- We have Sacred Scripture, sacred tradition, and the *fullness* of truth; we have endless delights! We could never plumb the depths of all of these treasures!

One gentleman who converted to Catholicism recently told me, "It's so *fun* to be Catholic!" He said this because he is really enjoying his exploration and discovery of these endless riches of our faith.

In this chapter, we will be discussing another beautiful way of coming to Christ and finding refreshment and peace — Adoration. Pope Emeritus Benedict XVI said: "Adoration is to enter into profound heartfelt communion with the Lord who makes

This is a quiet beach near my house where we filmed this third episode. During my childhood, I spent many summer days with my brothers and sisters enjoying this peaceful beauty.

himself bodily present in the Eucharist!" (Meeting with Priests of the Rome Diocese, March 2, 2006).

To me personally, this theme of "Coming to Christ" and resting in His love *primarily* calls to mind Adoration, where we come before our Lord exposed in the Most Blessed Sacrament and commune with Him. Jesus said: **"Come to me, all you who labor and are burdened, and I will give you rest.... And you will find rest for yourselves"** (Matthew 11:28,29). A holy hour of Adoration is spending time with our Lord, *basking* in His presence and soaking up His peace, beauty, goodness, and love. The word "bask" means "to expose oneself to pleasant warmth," like lying in the sun on a beautiful beach. Except in this case, we expose ourselves to the pleasant warmth of Christ's love for us, and His love doesn't burn; it's soothing and healing.

I thought it was an amazing "coincidence" as I was preparing this material that when I went to look up the official meaning of the word "bask" in the dictionary, I "just happened" to open up my 1,536-page dictionary to the *exact* page of the word "bask"! Wow! I sensed that our Lord really wanted me to tell you what *basking* in His love means! Let's put ourselves in the physical presence of the Son of God — and expose ourselves to the infinite goodness and warmth of the Sacred Heart of Jesus.

Saint Faustina said: "God is Love, and His Spirit is Peace" (*Diary*, 589). I have never once spent time in Adoration without coming out of the chapel filled with PEACE. Jesus gives us peace that the *world* cannot give. It is Christ's own peace. And it is priceless, especially in today's restless world.

On June 2, 2013, just days before this series was filmed in Maine, millions of people around the world celebrated Eucharistic Adoration together, led by Pope Francis. The Holy Father requested that the following intentions be remembered:

> For the Church spread throughout the world and united today in the adoration of the most holy Eucharist as a sign of unity. May the Lord make her ever more obedient to hearing his word in order to stand before the world "ever more beautiful, without stain or blemish, but holy and blameless." That through her faithful announcement, the Word that saves may still resonate as the bearer of mercy and may increase love to give full meaning to pain and suffering, giving back joy and serenity.

Our Holy Father's prayer intention reminds me that Mother Teresa said that every minute that we spend with our Lord in Eucharistic Adoration will deepen our union with Him and make our soul "everlastingly more glorious and beautiful in heaven, and will help bring about an everlasting peace on earth."

About four years ago, my younger sister Ruthie was going through an incredibly stressful and sorrowful time in her marriage. It was a very rough journey for her, to put it mildly. She always had gone to Mass on Sunday and she had said her prayers every day and night with her two children. But for the last couple of years, Ruthie started going to Adoration once a week. She said, "I go to get strength and peace." And she *gets* it! It is so beautiful to witness! When my sister started going through this ordeal, I didn't know how she was surviving, how she could even endure one day of her personal agony, and yet now, with Jesus, she is living with this beautiful serenity and freshness.

Last Christmas, Ruthie kept telling me: I have so much peace and joy inside. She could *feel* it! Even now when she has a rough day and has gotten upsetting news about something, she can go to Jesus and come out of that Adoration chapel imbued with a heavenly grace and peace. I'm telling you, we have a TREASURE here in the Catholic Church — and His name is Jesus. Our Lord Jesus is called the "treasure of the faithful."

Just last year, Ruthie shared with me that in the chapel she "cried and cried" as she knelt before our Lord at Adoration — but He consoled her. She said: "He fills you with that happiness and peace, so that you don't get all churned up inside. It's not that everything changes in your life — but He makes it all better. Adoration is the best way." She kept saying: "He *fills* you. Things go wrong every day, but He fills you with the graces to get *through* it all." You can "vent or listen or cry — whatever you need to do — you come out feeling so much better, and there's a *reason* for that; it's because you're giving it to Him. You see, most people, when they're all upset, are just passing that on to everyone else." Give it to Jesus instead! He can take it. In return, He gives you His blessed peace. All we have to do is come to Him, the Friend of our soul.

Each time we come to our Lord in Adoration is a chance to have a heart-to-heart with the King of Heaven. We are going to

Page 5: Wedding photograph of Susan's mom and dad.

Page 6: "The people who sit in darkness / have seen a great light, / on those dwelling in a land overshadowed by death / light has arisen" (Matthew 4:16).

Page 8: Filming the first segment of the Coming to Christ *series.*

Page 12: Setting up for filming the Coming to Christ *series.*

Page 15: Filming at Portland Head Light in Cape Elizabeth, Maine.

Page 17: We filmed one episode on a grassy peninsula at the end of these rocks, near these little fishermen's shacks overlooking the sea. Our Lord said to Saint Peter that he was "rock," and "upon this rock I will build my church" (Matthew 16:18). May we, too, cherish a rock-solid faith in Jesus Christ!

Page 20: One segment of the series was filmed within view of this simple sandy beach in Maine. I delight in the fact that God made that beautiful ocean and those islands offshore, and that soft sand and the gorgeous sky and those sweet-smelling, white sea roses.

Page 24: A gentle sunset at the beach where we taped our third episode of Coming to Christ.

Page 37: The brilliant morning sun rising over the horizon at Portland Head Light in Maine, where we filmed the first episode of Coming to Christ.

Page 38: We taped the second episode of Coming to Christ *at the refreshing Atlantic Ocean in my beloved home state of Maine.*

Page 43: One of the set of lighthouses at Two Lights State Park in Cape Elizabeth, Maine.

Page 45: Filming this episode on the Holy Mass was done in view of these two lighthouses overlooking the enormous expanse of open ocean.

Page 48: As we taped this second episode, I could see this lighthouse before me and the open Atlantic Ocean right beside me. I was sitting on the rugged rocks along the shore.

Page 58: Filming at sunrise on the beautiful coast of Maine, along the Atlantic Ocean.

Page 55: The morning sun rising over the open Atlantic Ocean at Two Lights State Park in Maine. This was our view as we filmed this second episode of Coming to Christ.

Page 61: This is a quiet beach near my house where we filmed this third episode. During my childhood, I spent many summer days with my brothers and sisters enjoying this peaceful beauty.

Page 68: The sun was rising over the ocean as we filmed this third presentation on a grassy peninsula overlooking distant lighthouses, islands, forts, and the open sea.

Page 76: Portland Head Light is seen in the distance, with simple fishermen's shacks on the grassy peninsula along the quiet shore. This is where we taped the third episode of Coming to Christ *early in the morning as the sun was rising over the ocean.*

Page 78: Open wilderness overlooking Mount Katahdin in Benedicta, Maine, where we taped the final two episodes of Coming to Christ.

Page 80: A glimpse of Mount Katahdin in Maine. This is our tallest peak and one of the first places in America where the sunlight touches each day.

Page 86: A beautiful, open field overlooking Mount Katahdin in Benedicta, Maine.

Page 87: Heavy chains, symbolic of our sins, hanging on a post of the front porch of a simple log cabin where we filmed the fourth episode. The beautiful open field, in stark contrast, could symbolize the glorious freedom of God's children, forgiven and redeemed by faithfully coming to Christ.

Page 95: Saint Benedict Church in Benedicta, Maine.

Page 97: The open sky and wide-open wilderness overlooking Mount Katahdin in Benedicta, Maine.

Page 98: View of Mount Katahdin.

Page 103: A view of the open land and distant mountains, as seen from the quiet town of Benedicta, Maine, where we taped the final two episodes of Coming to Christ.

Page 111: Mount Katahdin in the distance with a field of spring flowers.

Page 108: The quiet beauty of Maine. We filmed the final two episodes in front of this simple log cabin as we enjoyed the natural goodness of life all around us.

Page 115: Sun setting over Mount Katahdin and continuing its course across our country as we filmed our final episode of Coming to Christ.

Page 119: A beautiful sunrise on Willard Beach.

meet Jesus at the end of time, and we have all these beautiful opportunities to meet with Him now, as *often* as we wish. As often as we will quiet ourselves, go into a chapel where He is always waiting for us, and then walk out with peace.

Saint John Bosco said: "Make frequent visits to Jesus in the Blessed Sacrament and the devil will be powerless against you." The devil *wants* you to get all churned up inside and full of anxiety — but Jesus instead gives you His heavenly peace.

Seek our Lord Jesus. This is "the greatest adventure" of our lives, as Saint Augustine tells us. Seek His presence and His holy face: "Seek and you will find" (Matthew 7:7). Psalm 53:3 says that God looks down from heaven upon the children of men to see if there is one who is wise and seeks God. We should go out of our way to find Him, like the three wise men did. In Deuteronomy 4:29, our Lord says that if we seek Him with all our heart, we will find Him.

We are made for finding Him. He made us; we belong to Him. When we kneel before Him in adoration, He is actually looking back at us! Saint John Vianney said, "Ah! If only we had the angels' eyes! Seeing our Lord Jesus here on that altar, and looking at us, how we should love Him!" It's amazing to realize that the Son of the living God is looking *back* at us as we kneel before Him in adoration!

Pope Francis, soon after we taped these shows for EWTN in 2013, spoke about starting anew with Christ and developing an ever-stronger love for Christ. He said, "When you visit the Lord, when you look at the tabernacle, what do you do? … do you let yourself be looked at by the Lord? … He looks at us and this is itself a way of praying." He said that even if you fall asleep before our Eucharistic Lord, "He is still looking at you."

He truly sees you, He is close to you, and He loves you. Our Holy Father concluded by asking, "Do I find time to remain in his presence, in silence, to be looked upon by him? Do I let his fire warm my heart? If the warmth of God, of his love, of his tenderness is not in our own hearts, then how can we, who are poor sinners, warm the heart of others?" (Address to Catechists, September 27, 2013). He encouraged us to be very close to Jesus, remaining attached to Him and talking to Him.

Saint Alphonsus Liguori said: "The sovereigns of the earth do not always grant audiences readily; on the contrary, the King of Heaven, hidden under the Eucharistic veil, is ready to receive anyone." His Divine Majesty will accept even the likes of *us*! He will do so *warmly*!

Jesus said to Saint Faustina: "Know that My Heart is mercy itself. From this sea of mercy, graces flow out upon the whole world. No soul that has approached Me has ever gone away unconsoled. All misery gets buried in the depths of My mercy, and every saving and sanctifying grace flows from this fountain" (*Diary*, 1777).

When Saint Faustina referred to herself as "such a miserable bundle of imperfections," Jesus said, "Be at peace … it is precisely through such misery that I want to show the power of My Mercy" (*Diary*, 133).

I was quite stunned when I learned that Saint Peter Julian Eymard went so far as to say that "Eucharistic Adoration is the most necessary mission to the Church, which has even more need of prayerful souls than of powerful preachers or men of eloquence." Wow.

I always love sharing the beautiful and inspiring words of Mother Teresa about coming to Christ and adoring our Lord Jesus in the Most Holy Sacrament, spending time personally visiting the Son of God Himself! Mother Teresa said: "Nowhere on earth are you more welcomed, nowhere on earth are you more loved, than by Jesus, living and truly present in the Most Blessed Sacrament. The time you spend with Jesus in the Blessed Sacrament is the best time that you will spend on earth."

༄

I would like to turn now to a source of grace and peace that is available to us everywhere we go — a way to encounter Christ even in the privacy of our own home or even outdoors: PRAYER!

Prayer is an incredibly important topic. Prayer is a simple way of approaching our Lord Jesus always and everywhere.

Our Lord Jesus told Saint Faustina that "the prayer of a humble and loving soul … draws down an ocean of blessings" (*Diary*, 320). So, it is very meaningful to me to think about prayer with the beautiful ocean in the background!

The great Saint Teresa of Ávila said: "Give me a person who has fifteen minutes of mental prayer daily, and I will give you a saint." Just fifteen minutes a day of prayerful dialog with our Lord, loving attentiveness to God, being with Him in spirit and in truth — and you can become a saint.

The sun was rising over the ocean as we filmed this third presentation on a grassy peninsula overlooking distant lighthouses, islands, forts, and the open sea.

We come to Christ in our own heart and soul by stopping to look *within*. Saint Augustine said to our Lord: "You were within me, but I was not within *myself*." *Early on* in his life, Augustine was anywhere but within himself! The outside world has so many attractions that pull us all *away* from prayer. We can stay so busy and preoccupied with worldly distractions that we don't give our Lord a chance. We don't give Him any quality time and attention. My dad used to warn us not to get too caught up in things of this world so as to forget God and the things of *eternal* importance. It is so important for us to slow down and *recollect* — to gather ourselves together, to reel ourselves in, to gather our thoughts, and to put ourselves in the presence of the living God and talk with Him. Our King is waiting — but we just keep putting Him on hold. As my father used to say, remember God, and He will remember you.

We spend so many hours a day *deliberately* surrounding ourselves with noisy radio, television and all sorts of electronics and frivolous conversations — and if there was ever a time to *quiet* ourselves and attain a deep inner peace and inner strength through prayer, it is NOW.

Mother Teresa said that prayer is "oneness with Christ." That is what this *entire* book is all about — drawing nearer to Jesus and becoming ONE with Him. This is our destiny! This is our supreme good: knowing and gaining Jesus Christ — and being found in Him!

My sister Ruthie told me that even when she is at the office, she takes a minute to look over at the "Serenity Prayer" pinned to her wall and she silently prays it during the day. God is always there as an endless source of grace and peace in our lives — even when we're at work! We just have to take time to turn to Him and re-turn to Him in order to be refreshed, rejuvenated, and pacified.

Saint Teresa of Ávila also said that "some books on prayer tell us where one must seek God" — and then she added: "Within oneself, very clearly, is the best place to look."

Saint Faustina likewise said: "I do not look for Him outside myself" (*Diary*, 883). She even said that "nothing disturbs my union with the Lord, neither conversation with others nor any duties; even if I am to go about settling very important matters, this does not disturb me. My spirit is with God, and my interior being is filled with God, so I do not look for Him outside my-self" (*Diary*, 883).

One time when Saint Faustina was feeling "crushed" by "dreadful sufferings," from the bottom of her soul she prayed: "Do with me what You will, O Jesus; I will adore You in every-thing. May Your Will be done in me, O my Lord and my God, and I will praise Your infinite mercy" (*Diary*, 78). Through this simple prayer, this simple act of humble submission to God, the terrible torments left her. Suddenly she saw Jesus Who said to her: "I am always in your heart" (*Diary*, 78).

When we come to our Lord Jesus in prayer and loving at-tentiveness to Him, we find more serenity and calmness within our own heart. We can be freed of terrible torments, just like Saint Faustina was when she stopped to pray. Peace is the legacy that Christ leaves us. **"My peace I give to you,"** He said (John 14:27).

Saint Seraphim of Sarov said, "Acquire inner peace and thousands around you will find salvation."

৵

When it comes to acquiring peace in our hearts, I like what Father Jacques Philippe shared in his little book called *Searching for and Maintaining Peace.* He said:

Consider the surface of a lake, above which the sun is shining. If the surface of the lake is peaceful and tranquil, the sun will be reflected in this lake; and the more peace-ful the lake, the more perfectly will it be reflected. If, on the other hand, the surface of the lake is agitated, undulating, then the image of the sun cannot be reflected in it. (It is all broken apart and scattered.) It is a little bit like this with regard to our soul in its relationship with God. The more our soul is peaceful and tranquil, the more God is reflected in it, the more His image expresses itself in us, and the more His grace acts through us.

Don't let anyone or anything diminish your prayer life or steal your peace. If you lose your calm, come to Christ and get it back again. Live in His presence and draw great courage and inner strength from the sure knowledge that He is looking at you, He is supporting you, and He loves you. As my dad used to say, "I don't know *why* God loves us so much — but I know that He *does!*"

A priest named Father Pichon wrote to Saint Thérèse: "There is nothing more precious than your great peace. Don't allow the enemy to break into it. Listen to Jesus saying to *you* as to His intimate friends: Peace be with you!" He also told Saint Thérèse to "be very grateful and guard this gift from God."

༄

One of the very important aspects of drawing near to God and being filled with His peace is that the world depends on it. Our families depend on it. We need to be about the business of saving souls and getting our loved ones (and ourselves) safely home to everlasting life in heaven. We can't do that so well in a state of restlessness and anxiety. In the end, getting us all safely home to God is all that matters. And Jesus is the way. So now more than ever, we should be drawing closer to Christ, soaking up His peace, and pleading for the graces our families need for salvation, knowing that every heartfelt prayer is heard and answered.

Prayer gives us peace because it puts us in contact with our God of peace; Adoration gives us peace because we are basking in the sacred presence of the Prince of Peace; and I want to add that trusting more in God gives us peace, too.

The more we place our trust in God and have faith in Him, the more we can let go of our *useless* anxieties and fears and finally experience the rest and tranquility that our Lord promised to those who come to Him. Jesus said that fear is useless; what is needed is *trust* (cf. Mark 5:36).

I remember caring for my beautiful mother when she was dying of cancer. My heart was completely breaking. I was her primary caregiver, yet I couldn't take away all her suffering and I couldn't save her life. It was such a heavy burden of responsibility and it was *crushing* me. I actually thought I might die from the heartache and sorrow. And it must have shown on my face, because seeing the stress and sadness in my eyes while my sweet mother was dying, my dad said to me: "Don't worry, Susan; God governs everything." Those simple words of faith took an enormous and *unbearably* heavy weight off my shoulders.

Dad was exactly right. God governs everything. God is in control. We are just God's little helpers. We try to help Him in whatever way we can, and serve Him with all our ability and love in caring for one another, but God is managing everything and overseeing everything. He is carrying the heavy weight. He does all the heavy lifting. We just need to have more faith and try not to worry so much — just do the best we can and let God do the rest. Things work out much better if we can remain at peace.

In more recent years, I brought my 85-year-old dad to a doctor's appointment and together we were told point-blank by the doctor that he was dying. I was devastated by this news. It hit me like a ton of bricks. On the drive home from the doctor's office, I asked my father what he thought of the news, and he replied: "This isn't earth-shaking; this is natural." And I thought to myself: *Oh yeah.* He was right. When you're almost 86 years old, this is natural. And he was so calm about it, and so strong inside.

Every day and night I took care of him, and when it got close to the end, when my precious dad was close to dying, I asked him in the middle of the night while getting his medicine for him: "Dad, are you afraid?" And he answered: "No, not in the *least.* I know that God knows me." Dad had walked so closely with God all his life; he had talked to God every day. God knew my dad personally. And my dad had nothing to fear, not even death itself. I never knew any human being more at peace with God than my dad. And it came from a life of constant, heartfelt prayer.

Saint Augustine said, "If you pray well, you will live well. If you live well, you will die well. And if you die well, all will be well." That was my dad. *His* was one of the holiest deaths I have ever known.

స

I want to tell you about a dream that Saint Faustina had: Saint Thérèse appeared to her and told her that she needed to trust more in God (*Diary*, p. 84). Saint Faustina was still a novice at the time and was going through some difficulties that she did not know how to overcome. She made novenas to various saints, but the situation grew more and more difficult. The sufferings it caused her were so great that she did not know how to go on living. Suddenly it occurred to her that she should pray to Saint Thérèse of the Child Jesus. Before entering the convent she had a great devotion to her. Lately she had somewhat neglected this devotion, but in her dire need she began again to pray with great fervor.

On the fifth day of the novena, she dreamed of Saint Thérèse, but Thérèse hid from Faustina that she was a saint and began to comfort her, saying that she should not be worried about this matter, but should trust more in God. Thérèse said, "I suffered greatly too," but Faustina did not quite believe her and said, "It seems to me that you have not suffered at all." Thérèse answered that she had suffered *very much indeed* and told Faustina, "Know that in three days the difficulty will come to a happy conclusion." When Faustina was not very willing to believe her, she revealed that she was a saint. At that moment, a great joy filled Faustina's soul. Thérèse said again: "Trust that this matter will be resolved in three days." Saint Faustina started asking her questions, like: "Shall I go to heaven?" Thérèse answered, "Yes, you will go to heaven."

"And will I be a saint?" She replied, "Yes, you will be a saint."

"But little Thérèse, shall I be a saint as you are, raised to the altar?"

She answered, "Yes, you will be a saint just as I am, but you must trust in the Lord Jesus."

Faustina then asked her if her mother and father would go to heaven, and she replied that they would.

She further asked, "And will my brothers and sisters go to heaven?" Thérèse told Faustina to pray hard for them, but gave no definite answer. Faustina understood that they were in need of *much* prayer.

Faustina said that "three days later the difficulty was solved very easily, just as Thérèse had said." Keep in mind that this was a matter that was SO difficult and painful to Faustina that she didn't know how to overcome it and she didn't know how to go on *LIVING!* Yet it was resolved "very easily" after she was told to "trust more in God" and "trust in the Lord Jesus." Faustina noticed that everything in this affair turned out *exactly* as Thérèse said it would. "It was a dream, but it had its significance." Of course, Faustina is a saint — raised to the altar!

This story reminds us that the power of prayer is inconceivable. If only we knew! We would never stop praying!

I want to share one more quick point. Faustina was allowed to make a home visit for the first time in ten years when her mother was dying, and a lot of her brothers and sisters were grown up after all that time. She shared that she was very sorry not to have seen two of her sisters during that home visit. She felt interiorly that their souls were in great danger. Pain gripped her heart just at the thought of them. Once, when she felt very close to God, she fervently asked the Lord to grant them grace, and our Lord answered her: "I am granting them not only necessary graces, but special graces as well" (*Diary*, 401). Faustina understood that the Lord would call them to a *greater union* with Himself. Look at the GENEROSITY of Jesus! We give so *little* to God — our simple prayers — and He in return gives so MUCH! Such an outpouring of grace, mercy and blessings! This is the way it is with God. We give so little, and He gives so much. He gives us everything.

After Mom was called home to heaven, we found a little poem in her handwriting. These words of faith in God meant a lot to our mother, who was one of the most serene, peaceful and trusting human beings I have ever met. The poem is called "THERE'S A REASON":

Portland Head Light is seen in the distance, with simple fishermen's shacks on the grassy peninsula along the quiet shore. This is where we taped this third episode of Coming to Christ *early in the morning as the sun was rising over the ocean.*

For every pain that we must bear,
For every burden, every care,
There's a Reason.

For every grief that bows the head,
For every teardrop that is shed,
There's a Reason.

For every hurt, for every plight,
For every lonely pain-racked night,
There's a Reason.

But if we trust God as we should,
It *all* will work out for our good.
He knows the Reason.

Open wilderness overlooking Mount Katahdin in Benedicta, Maine, where we taped the final two episodes of Coming to Christ.

ॐ

Chapter 4

CONFESSION

Throughout this book we have been discussing how to come to our Lord Jesus, be filled with His peace, and rest in His divine love. It is important for us to know how to find the Messiah, because there are *eternal* consequences of finding Him or not finding Him. "No one comes to the Father" except through Jesus (John 14:6). He is our bridge to heaven. That is what our Heavenly Father said to Saint Catherine of Siena: The road to heaven was broken by the sin and disobedience of Adam in such a way that no one could arrive at eternal life. So, God our Father, wishing to remedy our great evils, gave us the bridge of His Son in order that, passing across the flood, we may not be drowned or swept away — and He referred to this flood as "the tempestuous sea of this dark life." God is telling us to take the remedy and look at the greatness of this bridge that reaches from earth to heaven!

God said to Saint Catherine: "Look at the bridge of My only-begotten Son." He is basically saying: Behold the Lamb of

A glimpse of Mount Katahdin in Maine.
This is our tallest peak and one of the first places in
America where the sunlight touches each day.

God! Come to Christ. He is your *lifeline*! Only in this way will we be restored to a life of grace and brought safely home to heaven. Always remember that Jesus is the bridge. His holy cross formed the bridge to eternal life. We should walk *speedily* on it, our Heavenly Father said! How great is the gift of our Lord's adorable and innocent Blood, which paid the price of our salvation and paved the way to eternal life.

Benedicta, Maine, is called "God's country"! This is the only town in all of Maine that was founded by a Catholic bishop. Benedict Fenwick was the Bishop of Boston in the early 1800s, and he wanted to establish a Catholic farming community in rural Maine to help people from the larger cities in New England to seek a new life away from the temptations and spiritual dangers of city life. This peaceful, quiet town — established specifically as a community of faith — attracted very healthy and virtuous Catholics. Many were Irish families who wanted to live in the countryside, and some of them actually traveled from Boston to Benedicta on foot! Those were very sturdy early settlers who came here and "sought their joy in God and nature."

Being surrounded by the simple quiet beauty of Maine makes it easier to focus on how to find Christ by coming to Him in the confessional! This topic should not scare any of us away, because it is too beautiful and important.

My college-age nephew Matthew recently told me: "I know for sure that I share three things in common with all saints: I was born, I will die, and I have sinned. I'm off to a good start," he said, "so now I just need to fill in the blanks and I'll be there in no time!"

It is true. Matthew is right that each one of us alive today was born. Each one of us will die. Each one of us has sinned. But the saints did something beyond this, something *different* from what everyone else was doing — they became holy, in spite of their personal weaknesses and failings. They didn't *settle* for just worldly and sinful lives; instead they sought to fulfill their *highest* potential and reach their *highest* dignity as children of God, made in the image and likeness of God. They decided to "go for the gold," so to speak — to amend their lives, to change their sinful ways, to cooperate with God, to receive His forgiveness, and to really work with the Lord for His holy purposes. They sought to have their souls washed clean and restored to their original beauty — and having done so, they are now touching the world for endless ages as a result of what God did *with* them and what God did *through* them.

Our Heavenly Father said to Saint Catherine of Siena, "though I created you without your help, I will not save you without it" (*Dialogues*, 23). We really have to *work* with the Lord to attain the great heights of holiness and heaven.

If Saint Augustine had remained steeped in sin, we would not be talking about him today. We would not even *know* him. He would have disappeared into oblivion and possibly even into hell. Instead, he turned back to God, from Whom we came and to Whom we should be returning. You could say that Augustine finally began to rest in God's love. Augustine is the one who said to our Lord: "My soul is restless until it rests in *You*." He finally let God have His way with him and he became a great saint.

Likewise, if Saint Paul had continued on his sinful way of persecuting and killing Christians, following his own passions and ideas instead of God's will and holy purposes, we wouldn't know *Saint* Paul, and he wouldn't be the great saint that he is.

If Mother Teresa had refused to obey God's will in leaving everything she loved to serve the poorest of the poor in India, you and I wouldn't know anyone by the name of "Blessed Teresa of Calcutta."

And the list goes on and on.

Mother Teresa used to say: If you are already a saint, *thank God*. If you are a sinner, don't remain one. It's as simple as that. If the saints had *remained* in their lives of sin and selfishness, following their own whims and fancies, they would be just like everybody else in the world and they wouldn't be saints. But we are *all* called to be saints — we are called to a FAR better life than what we ourselves can even imagine — a far more beautiful, loving, joy-filled, and fruitful life. In fact, *eternal* life!

Let's let the saints inspire us to turn our lives around and start looking at God *full-facedly*. Every time we sin, we turn our *backs* to God. When we repent, we turn our *faces* to Him again.

Mother Angelica of EWTN once said: "Holiness is a beautiful struggle!" I *love* that! Let's begin to really engage in this beautiful struggle to become holy! It is not easy, but it is beautiful — and it is so worthwhile. In fact, it is the most worthwhile pursuit of our lives.

We would do well always to remember that "every saint has a past, and every sinner has a future." We should never be discouraged, never lose hope. When we read the lives of the saints and some of their less-than-stellar track records, we realize that there is hope for us *all*! Every single one of us. God can transform even the most rebellious sinners into the most remarkable saints. As long as we come to Christ and really begin to *work* with Him.

As we reflect upon Confession, I want us to recall how Saint Peter the Apostle, *who was a sinner just like us, wept* over his sins. He really grieved over having offended such a good and loving Lord. Where is *our* sorrow for sin today? Where is our sadness at offending our good God Whom we love and Who loves us so dearly? That is an important part of repentance — and repentance is *key* to salvation. Remember how our Lord Jesus said, **"Weep ... for yourselves and for your children"** (Luke 23:28). Even though Jesus was the one suffering and enduring a bitter Passion at that moment, He told them: "Do not weep for me" but rather for *yourselves*. Weep for your sins and for the sins of your children.

In Luke 1:76-77, the prophet Zechariah, the father of Saint John the Baptist, exclaimed: "And you, child, will be called prophet of the Most High, / for you will go before the Lord to prepare his ways, / to give his people knowledge of salvation."

HOW? How was John to give God's people knowledge of salvation? "Through the forgiveness of their sins" (Luke 1:77). We can't be saved without the forgiveness of our sins. We can't get to heaven without acknowledging and then turning *away* from our sinful behaviors, turning to God for mercy, and having our stains *washed away*. We have to be pardoned and have our baptismal robes washed *clean* again before we can live forever in the presence of our holy, holy, holy Lord.

That's why John and Jesus cried out to the people: "RE-PENT!" They preached repentance for the forgiveness of sins. And when our Lord encountered someone who had been engaging in sins of the flesh, He mercifully told her, **"Go, [and] from now on do not sin any more"** (John 8:11). Don't do that anymore. Change your lifestyle. *That's* repentance. Both Jesus and John preached *cleaning up* our lives and changing our ways — so that we can recognize love when He is standing right in front of us. Sin blinds us to the truth. We need a PURE heart so that we can see God.

If we would really *love* the Lord our God and start looking through *His* eyes of wisdom, we would develop a strong hatred of sin and a great love of virtue. Jesus spoke in pretty dramatic language about the importance of stopping our sinful behavior right away. He said, **"If your hand causes you to sin, cut it off ... if your foot causes you to sin, cut it off ... if your eye causes you to sin, pluck it out. Better for you to enter into the kingdom of God with one eye [hand/ foot] than with two eyes [hands/feet] to be thrown into Gehenna, where 'their worm does not die, and the fire is not quenched"** (Mark 9:43-48). Jesus is telling us that the consequences of sin are *deadly* serious, and we should be taking serious action to avoid it at all costs. Cut off from yourself all access to the source of temptation in your life. Starting now, *going forward*, do everything in your power to avoid the near occasions of sin. If you fall into sin, return to a state of grace as quickly as possible. Seek "the warmth of God's mercy," as Saint Bernardine of Siena tells us.

Coming to Jesus in the Sacrament of Confession is one of the most powerful ways to receive *super-abundant grace* for practicing virtue and *divine assistance* for turning away from vice. One of my friends here in Maine refers to the Sacrament of Recon-

*A beautiful, open field overlooking Mount Katahdin
in Benedicta, Maine.*

ciliation as "going to the garbage collector." I never thought of
Confession quite like that before, but it does make sense. Let all
our sins be carried away and completely disposed of, never to be
seen again, completely forgotten by Christ! We can start fresh.
Out with the bad, in with the good!

Saint Padre Pio used to say that even an unoccupied room
collects dust, so we must regularly confess our sins and regularly
have our souls washed clean in this beautiful Sacrament, to keep
ourselves a fit abode for His Divine Majesty.

Confession is simply coming back to Christ with total honesty so "that your sins may be wiped away, and that the Lord may
grant you times of refreshment" (Acts 3:19-20).

Jesus said to Saint Faustina:

... even if the sins of souls were as dark as night, when the sinner turns to My Mercy, he gives Me the greatest praise and is the glory of My Passion. When a soul extols My goodness, Satan trembles before it and flees to the very bottom of hell. (*Diary*, 378)

Heavy chains, symbolic of our sins, hanging on a post of the front porch of a simple log cabin where we filmed this fourth episode. The beautiful open field, in stark contrast, could symbolize the glorious freedom of God's children, forgiven and redeemed by faithfully coming to Christ.

I think that's *awesome!* We actually can make the devil run away from us and flee to the depths of hell just by turning to God's mercy, trusting in His loving kindness, praising His infinite goodness and seeking the priceless gift of His forgiveness as often as we need it.

Our Lord said to Saint Faustina: "Mankind will not have peace until it turns to the Fount of My Mercy" (*Diary*, 699).

$$\wp$$

Jesus compared His mercy to an enormous expanse of ocean — the ocean of Divine Mercy! We throw our sins in there and they are never seen again. All gone! Jesus is "the Lamb of God Who *takes away* the sins of the world." He takes *away* our sins. They disappear in the ocean of His love. But we've got to come to Him and give Him all that we want Him to take away.

Our Holy Father Pope Francis said that Jesus never tires of forgiving us — it's we who get tired of *asking* for forgiveness.

Some people tell me they've had a bad experience in the confessional and they weren't told what they wanted to hear from the priest — and as a result, they hadn't gone back to Confession, even for *years*. All I can say is: Go again! It's way too important. Have the faith, humility, and sincerity to go again. Do it for love of Jesus and for eternal salvation. Don't ever let pride or hurt feelings get in the way. There's too much at stake.

I think it is important to be reminded again and again that our Lord Jesus said to Saint Faustina that **"only the humble soul is able to receive My grace"** (*Diary*, 1220). Each time we participate in the Sacrament of Reconciliation, we place ourselves in a *humble* posture as we kneel before our Lord in the confessional, and we *humbly* acknowledge our faults and failures. What does Jesus do in response to this act of humility and trust on our part? He *absolves* us of our iniquities, washes our souls, and takes an enormous load off our shoulders. That heavy weight of sin is just *taken* from us! Many of you understand what it's like to come out of the confessional feeling a hundred pounds *lighter*! This is the peace of being forgiven an enormous debt. It is so *freeing*! It is priceless. You can't *buy* that kind of peace, even with all the money in the world. That's how precious Christ's peace is — the peace that comes with the forgiveness of our sins.

Before going into the confessional, I like to ask our Blessed Mother to please help me to make a good, honest, and sincere confession, to help me "come clean"! Ask Our Lady and the Holy Spirit for the clarity and the courage to see and acknowledge all our faults and defects, and own up to them, and also for the grace to change for the better — for that "firm purpose of amendment," as we call it. *Drop* the boulder, as my friend says. Stop carrying around unnecessary burdens that Jesus can *easily* take from you! Let Him lighten your load. Let Him absolve and strengthen your heart and soul and grant you that glorious freedom of God's children. Freedom from *sin*. That's what He came for: to free us from our slavery to sin and the oppressive weight of our own faults and failings.

When the Lamb of God takes away your sins, you will not only be filled with much more *peace*, but you will also have a much greater capacity for JOY. But it is imperative that we acknowledge our sins and get rid of the "trash." Let it go. Again,

Jesus is the collector. As they say, a clear conscience is a *very* soft pillow, which is conducive to rest and peace, which is what this book is all about coming to Christ and finding rest.

Saint Bernadette said that "sin is the greatest disaster." If we only knew how it defiles and deforms us inside, if we could see what it does to our souls, we'd stop sinning right away. If we want to avert *further* disaster in our lives and make everyone's life a little easier, we should not only partake sincerely of the Sacrament of Confession, but also really strive for virtue now. I don't think we half realize the awfulness of sin and all the negative consequences of sin in our lives; otherwise, we would be filled with a *horror* of sin.

We have this *amazing* tendency as human beings to justify our sins and excuse everything we do. I have listened to people tell of their terribly dark and sinful behaviors — even *mortal* sins — and justify it all by pointing out that others do *worse*! Do not compare yourselves to others; otherwise, you will think you are a saint when in reality you are still a very poor sinner. Compare yourself ONLY to Jesus Christ and to our Blessed Mother Mary. Use the highest standards of measurement, not the lowest standards — which sadly is what most people use. Always remember how Jesus said that the road to eternal damnation is wide and *many* go that way, while the road to heaven is rough and narrow and few are those who find it. Don't justify your sinful behavior by comparing it to what other people are doing in this cesspool of a culture, so filled with the corruption of selfishness and serious immorality.

According to our Heavenly Father in His words to Saint Catherine of Siena, the sin of impurity is a great CRUELTY —

a cruelty to ourselves and a cruelty to those with whom we engage in this sin — because it does such damage to souls, destroying the precious life of grace in us, and it offends our *infinitely good God* who calls us to be holy even as He is holy.

We should ask ourselves every day: Would God approve of everything I did today? Would God be pleased with everything that I just said and did? Nothing else matters more than what God thinks of our actions. That is why I love the sign that Mother Teresa had in her convent in the South Bronx: "Jesus is the silent Listener at every conversation." God hears everything we say and sees everything we do, and we would do well to stay mindful of that. "The LORD, your God, is in your midst" (Zephaniah 3:17).

In our adult years, our dad would tell us ten children: "None of us are saints; get to Confession," and we couldn't argue with that. He was right.

Saint Ignatius gave us the advice to turn to Our Lady so "that she may obtain grace for us from her Son … an understanding of the disorder of our actions, that filled with *horror* of them, we may amend our life and put it in order." I shared this quotation with my beloved dad one time, and he was very touched by it. He said that we can amend our life and put it in order "with our Blessed Mother's grace, with her strength."

Dad said:

That's a saint — the *making* of a saint. That's the whole secret of sanctity. You'll be a saint if you do it. Ask Our Lady to *show* you your faults. She will tell you in your mind "don't do that — what you did yesterday." She will make you aware. She will give you the awareness of what is wrong, and the grace to *overcome* it. That's the secret to heaven right there. That's the key. Without [Christ, her Son], we can do nothing: We can't even *breathe*. Ask Our Lady to give us the grace to know what's wrong. Only then can we *fix* it — with the help of God's grace. To *know* our sins and weaknesses and to *amend* them — there's the answer about how to be holy, how to be perfect.

If we do the important work of amending our lives now, then we won't need to spend quite as much time in purgatory. We should aim for the highest heaven, because as humans, we tend to fall a little short of our desired goals. If we're only aiming for purgatory and we miss it even just by a *little* bit, we're in big trouble. Aim *much higher* than purgatory. Do your purgatory now. Purify your lives and souls now. Repent, as Jesus says.

I want to share with you this heartfelt prayer from my dad. He prayed:

Blessed Mother, give me the grace — help me to be aware of where I can *improve*, and give me the strength, and grace, and wisdom, and knowledge to do it. Take my hand and give me the understanding of what I'm doing wrong and the grace to do everything *right*.

After saying this prayer from his heart, my dad turned to me and said: "If you do it, you're a saint. If we could only do what we know we should."

When we step into the confessional to acknowledge our sins and failures, it is good to remember that our Lord Jesus told Saint Faustina that He Himself is there, hidden by the priest. We confess our sins to *Jesus Himself,* and we are washed and forgiven by *Jesus Himself* in this Sacrament of Reconciliation. It is like approaching God's throne of MERCY. That's what He's dispensing! He is handing out forgiveness and grace, and as I keep telling you, it's all FREE! All we have to do is come! Come with honesty, humility, and a bit of faith. **"Come to me, all you who labor and are burdened, and I will give you rest"** (Matthew 11:28). I will give you peace, Jesus said.

Here are the actual words our Lord said to Saint Faustina:

When you go to confession, to this fountain of My mercy, the Blood and Water which came forth from My Heart always flows down upon your soul and ennobles it. Every time you go to confession, immerse yourself entirely in My mercy, with great trust, so that I may pour the bounty of My grace upon your soul. When you approach the confessional, know this, that I Myself am waiting there for you. I am only hidden by the priest, but I Myself act in your soul. Here the misery of the soul meets the God of mercy. Tell souls that from this fount of mercy souls draw graces solely with the vessel of trust. If their trust is great, there is no limit to My generosity. The torrents of grace inundate humble souls. The proud remain always in poverty and misery, because My grace turns away from them to humble souls. (*Diary*, 1602)

I once went to Confession to a very holy priest here in Maine, and after I confessed my failings, he felt moved and inspired by the Holy Spirit to give me a particular penance, which seemed unusual to him. He was behind a grille; he couldn't see me, but I could see him and he was rubbing his temples as he explained that he had never given this particular penance to *anyone* before. He seemed to be hesitating, but he said he felt compelled by the Holy Spirit to say these particular words of advice for my penance — and it *changed my life*. I'm telling you: Jesus is there! Just as Saint John Vianney would point to the tabernacle and tell his parishioners: "Jesus is there! He is there!" We too can point to the confessional and say: "Jesus is there!" He is there with great mercy and love. Come with great trust to His fountain of mercy!

Our Heavenly Father told Saint Catherine of Siena: "My mercy is greater without any comparison than all the sins which any creature can commit" (*Dialogue* 4.4.31). We should never think that our sin is greater than God's mercy and goodness, because that is impossible. To use Saint Catherine's words, even if our lives have been "disordered and wicked," we must "hope greatly" in His mercy and reach for His forgiveness in the confessional, and we will obtain it in *abundance*, more than we even know how to desire. "Though we are sinners, we trust in your mercy and love" (from the former Eucharistic Prayer I).

Let's trust not just a *little* bit, but *boundlessly* in the goodness of our God. He really loves that trust, and He is so worthy of it. I want our trust to *match* the amount of His mercy, which is INFINITE. Keep in mind this important concept: If you bring a *thimble size* amount of trust, He will fill you with graces according

Saint Benedict Church in Benedicta, Maine.

to the degree or measure of your trust. Your trust is like a *container* that gets filled with grace. If you bring a *cup*-size, He will fill that whole cup with blessings. If you bring a *big pail* of trust, He will fill it to the brim. Bring GREAT trust and you will receive great graces. Bring huge confidence in our Lord. Trust and believe. His love is like an OCEAN of mercy, so we should bring an *ocean-sized* TRUST.

Jesus said these words to St. Faustina: "The more a soul trusts, the more it will receive. Souls that trust boundlessly are a great comfort to Me, because I pour all the treasures of My graces into them. I rejoice that they ask for much, because it is My desire to give much, very much" (*Diary*, 1578).

In Sacred Scripture, we learn that God calls us to be "holy and without blemish" in His sight (Ephesians 5:27). That's a very tall order — and yet He cannot command the impossible, and He personally helps us to *achieve* it.

Our Lord said that souls who are striving for perfection should particularly adore His mercy, because the abundance of graces which He grants us flows from His mercy. He said: "I desire that these souls distinguish themselves by boundless trust in My mercy. I Myself will attend to the sanctification of such souls. I will provide them with everything they will need to attain sanctity" (*Diary*, 1578). WOW! Jesus will make us holy — He will take care of all of that for us. All we have to do is trust Him and come to Him.

My dad, even at the age of 85, kept going to Confession regularly — even though he didn't do much other than attend daily Mass, pray his Rosary, watch EWTN and the news, and enjoy an occasional John Wayne movie. We should stay very close to this beautiful Sacrament, even if our lives are simple. If only we knew the graces that fill us each time we come to Christ in this way!

Let me end this chapter with a very brief, but heartfelt prayer: "Jesus, I TRUST in You!"

The open sky and wide-open wilderness overlooking
Mount Katahdin in Benedicta, Maine.

View of Mount Katahdin.

∽

Chapter 5

JOY

Majestic Mount Katahdin is the tallest peak in our state of Maine. The name Katahdin means "greatest mountain," and the summit of Mount Katahdin is said to be one of the first places in America that the sunlight touches before spreading across our country — so it was very meaningful and symbolic that we were speaking in that particular location about coming to Christ, the light of the world, the light of our lives!

As the sun prepares to set over the mountains, it is easy to call to mind the importance of finding and sharing JOY! As Scripture keeps reminding us, rejoicing in the Lord should be our strength! (Nehemiah 8:10). Saint Paul tells us, **"Rejoice in the Lord always. I shall say it again: rejoice!"** (Philippians 4:4). Even our sweet Blessed Mother Mary — who barely says anything at all that is recorded in Sacred Scripture — couldn't help but exclaim, **"My spirit rejoices in God my savior"** (Luke 1:47). They say that joy is the infallible sign of God's presence. So, this is a very important topic! In finding Christ and drawing near to Him, we will find joy; in fact, we will find *everlasting* joy.

Psalm 34:6 tells us to look to Him that we may be radiant with joy! I have always loved that. Our joy comes from looking to our Lord and Savior!

I was very inspired when one of our priests here in Maine shared with us that not only the holy season of Lent but every season throughout the year should be a time for turning away from sin, drawing closer to God, and being filled with the Spirit of Christ. He said that it should be *more* than just a time of *fasting*: It should be a *joyous season of feasting*!

Every day we should:

- Fast from walking in the darkness; feast on *staying in the light*.

- Fast from discontent; feast on *gratitude*.

- Fast from anger; feast on *patience*.

- Fast from complaining; feast on *quiet acceptance* and *appreciation*.

- Fast from bitterness; feast on *forgiveness*.

- Fast from self-concern; feast on *compassion for others*.

- Fast from anxiety; feast on *trusting* in the divine providence of God.

- Fast from discouragement; feast on *hope*.

- Fast from laziness; feast on *commitment.*

- Fast from suspicion; feast on *truth.*

- Fast from idle talk and gossip; feast on *purposeful silence.*

- Fast from problems that overwhelm; feast on *prayer that strengthens.*

- Fast from the muddle of indecision; feast on *the word of God.*

- Fast from guilt; feast on *the mercy and forgiveness of God.*

- Fast from grimness; feast on *joy.*

And this leads very nicely into this topic of JOY!

You might remember from my previous television series or books that the very first words I ever read by Mother Teresa were words on joy. My mom had torn a page from a magazine with a beautiful painting of Mother Teresa and these words: "Joy is prayer. Joy is strength. Joy is love."

And joy is one of the actual requirements for becoming one of Mother Teresa's Missionaries of Charity. The sisters must have a spirit of cheerfulness, which is essential in that type of ministry in the darkest, poorest, and most suffering places on earth.

While I was with Mother Teresa's joy-filled sisters in Calcutta, every morning we were receiving our Lord Jesus and taking Him to heart in Holy Communion. Every day we were serving Jesus in His distressing disguise of the poor, the orphaned, and the dying. Every night we were adoring Jesus in the Most Blessed Sacrament. Morning, noon, and night, we were continually with Jesus, Jesus, Jesus. No wonder there was so much joy *in spite of how hard it was* in Calcutta. Our Lord said: **"Come to me, all you who labor and are burdened, and I will give you rest"** (Matthew 11:28). Our Lord sustains, refreshes, and rejuvenates us even during our hard labors. *Not only that,* but Jesus said clearly that there is more happiness in *giving* than in receiving. There is more joy in pouring ourselves out for one another than in keeping everything to ourselves.

I am especially touched by how our Lord said, **"As the Father loves me, so I also love you"** (John 15:9). Do we realize what He is *saying* here? As the Father loves JESUS CHRIST, His only-begotten Son in Whom He is well pleased, that is how much Jesus loves US! Wow. That is an enormous and very beautiful love! That's huge! The Father loves His Son Jesus very, *very* much! Infinitely and incomprehensively. That is how Jesus loves each one of us! I can't get over it. I am overwhelmed by the *enormity* and tenderness of Christ's love for us. I could cry for joy. Mother Teresa so wanted us to grasp our Savior's love for us that she encouraged us to say this little prayer repeatedly throughout the day and really let it sink into our hearts: "O my Jesus, I believe in Your tender, faithful love for me. I love You!"

Our Lord Jesus went *on* to say: **"Remain in my love. If you keep my commandments, you will remain in my love, just as I have kept my Father's commandments and remain in his love"** (John 15:9-10). Then He said some-

*A view of the open land and distant mountains, as seen
from the quiet town of Benedicta, Maine, where we
taped the final two episodes of* Coming to Christ.

thing very beautiful: **"I have told you this so that my joy may be in you and your joy may be complete"** (John 15:11). He wants us to share His joy completely — so that we will be filled with the fullness of divine happiness. And He tells us *how.* We are to keep His commandment of love: Love God above all, and love one another. Help one another. Forgive one another. Rescue and care for one another. Pray for one another. Be kind, loving, and gentle to one another. That's how we remain in His love and come to share in His divine JOY, the fullness of joy.

At the time of my first trip to Calcutta, I wrote this in my diary:

> I have never found any true, deep, inner happiness outside the context of love. LOVE and real inner joy have been *inseparable* for me. One does not *exist* without the other. Loving (God and loving) one another is what life is all about.

Saint Thérèse pointed out that "great love, not great deeds, is the essence of sanctity." It's always about the LOVE.

Mother Teresa said, "Joy comes to those who in a sense forget themselves and become totally aware of the other." Joy comes to those who learn to LOVE. This reminds me of something that I found fascinating about the behind-the-scenes life of the Missionaries of Charity. I first met Mother Teresa when I was 21 years old, and the following year, when I was 22, I was visiting with her in the South Bronx, New York. Mother told me to stay and live with the Sisters for a while. While living in the convent, brushing my teeth and getting ready for the day, I discovered that there were NO MIRRORS — even at the sink in the bathroom. There were *no mirrors at all,* and after a few days of not seeing myself, I actually started to *forget* myself! That was an amazing experience!

No wonder Mother Teresa was so humble — she barely ever saw herself, so she was never preoccupied with herself; instead, she was focused on God and others. There's JOY in that. Again, when we don't look at ourselves so much, we start to forget about ourselves — and that's a good thing. It is conducive to greater love, humility, and holiness. Remember how Saint Faustina said that "now I understand why there are so few saints; it is because so few souls are deeply humble" (*Diary,* 1306). If we would spend less time worrying about ourselves, and spend a little more time thinking about God and caring for one another, we could become more holy — and much more JOYFUL.

Blessed Francis Xavier Seelos, the saint of New Orleans, said: "If you want to be happy, be holy…. If you want to be very happy, be very holy."

Dr. Albert Schweitzer shared something similar when he said: "[T]he only ones among you who will be really happy are those who have sought and found how to serve." As Christians, we are called to imitate Christ in His way of love and virtue. We follow *Jesus,* and Jesus clearly told us that He came not to be served but to serve, and to give His Life as a ransom for many. No one is more blessed and happy than our Lord and Savior right now. He gave His all. He sacrificed everything for love of us. As followers of Christ, we should be experiencing the joy of loving through constant self-giving. As Mother Teresa said, we should "find ways to make others happy," and "Let no one ever come to you without leaving better and happier," because "life is the joy of loving and being loved."

In Calcutta, there was a young volunteer named Moira from Australia who was wonderful at working with children. She invited a small group of us to join her in putting on skits and mimes to entertain the lepers and destitute children in a village outside the city of Calcutta. I personally can't sing or dance worth beans, but in India, I sang and danced! I did anything I could to bring JOY to those in misery. We visited the lepers and entertained village children, and after we finished our songs and dances, we invited the people from the "audience" to come forward and share a song or dance. Three little girls came to the front of the room and shared a lovely Indian song and dance. I was very touched by how gracefully they moved their wrists and feet and heads as they sang. After they finished, the littlest girl came and tried to teach me how to dance Indian style. Little did I know that when I resumed my work in the Home for the Dying each afternoon back in the city of Calcutta, this would end up being a beautiful gift to share.

One afternoon as I was walking past a dark corner of the Home for the Dying, a poor woman reached up to me from her death bed for some water, and her wrist turned in such a way as to remind me of the children dancing in the village. So there in a dark corner of Mother Teresa's Home for the Dying, standing over this emaciated, dying woman's bed, I began to dance Indian style. Even though this poor woman had little or no life left in her even to lift her arm, and barely enough strength even to speak a word, when she saw me dancing, she started laughing and laughing! I still don't know whether to take that as a compliment or an insult, but I discovered that I could bring her JOY and take her mind off her misery, even with Indian dancing at its worst.

Always remember the importance of giving love and JOY to those around us. God loves a cheerful giver — not a grumpy one. Mother Teresa said that "joy is a net of love by which you can catch souls" and bring them to Christ, bring them to salvation. We won't win many souls for Christ and eternal life with a grimace on our face. We give most when we give with JOY.

To cultivate more joy in our hearts, I also feel that one of the secrets is very simply to appreciate all the wonderful blessings and all the simple joys in everyday life: our warm slippers, a hot cup of tea, a nice sunset, a soft pillow at night, a delicious ice cream from time to time! Be grateful, be grateful, be grateful! Thank God for *everything*: our food, clothing, shelter, family, faith, fresh air, everything we have. We are so blessed! We have so much. And if we are really honest with ourselves, all of us will acknowledge that we even have more than enough. As my dad used to say: "We're not half grateful enough."

I even like to thank God for GOD! I thank Him for being such a GOOD God. He is only ALL GOOD. Thank heavens for that. How merciful and kind He has been to us. He is our greatest benefactor.

*The quiet beauty of Maine. We filmed the final two episodes
in front of this simple log cabin as we enjoyed the natural
goodness of life all around us.*

Even if we are suffering, we should understand, as people of faith, that we are still so blessed because **"The LORD is close to the brokenhearted,"** and those who are crushed in spirit He saves (cf. Psalm 34:19). When I am at my lowest moments in life, those words give me so much comfort and consolation, because I always want to be close to God, and when we are suffering, He is really close to us. We are even more precious to Him. Also, during times of misery, I love to pray this verse inspired by Psalm 51: **"Give me back the JOY of Your salvation"** (cf. vs. 14). I really hold onto the word of God and find so much strength and grace therein.

Pope Francis told us that "a life without challenges does not exist." I was very edified by that dose of reality. Suffering is part of life. We can't run from it, so we might as well face it head-on — as peacefully, trustingly, and bravely as we can, for love of Jesus. We must undergo many hardships before we can enter the kingdom of God, as Saint Paul told us — and I *really* want to enter the kingdom of God.

Saint Padre Pio told us that we should "Bless the good God in everything," and "Bless Him in all that He makes you suffer and rejoice in it, for each victory gained has a corresponding crown in paradise." That's why the holy martyrs, even as they went to brutal torture and death, were singing hymns to God! They had joy because they had God. They had great love of God!

This ties in with what Saint Rose of Lima wrote:

Our Lord and Savior lifted up His voice and said with incomparable majesty: "Let all men know that grace comes after tribulation. Let them know that without the burden of afflictions it is impossible to reach the height of grace. Let them know that the gifts of grace increase as the struggles increase. Let men take care not to stray and be deceived. This is the only true stairway to paradise, and without the cross they can find no road to climb to heaven.... If only mortals would learn how great it is to possess divine grace, how beautiful, how noble, how precious. How many riches it hides within itself, how many joys and delights! No one would complain about his cross or about troubles that may happen to him, if he would come to know the scales on which they are weighed when they are distributed to men.

I think it is important for us to have a change of attitude and let our sufferings make us *better* — not bitter. Don't become a bitter old woman or a bitter old man because of all your sufferings — become BETTER because of them, like my grampa who suffered a lot throughout his entire life but was very kind. I know some people who have suffered more than most of us ever will in our whole lifetime, and yet *while we are complaining about our hardships,* they are becoming holy and humble and even more loving and kind because of them. They are at peace with God, which is such a beautiful and inspiring thing to witness.

I love to remind people that, "if God allows you to suffer much, it is because He has great designs for you, and He cer-

*Mount Katahdin in the distance with
a field of spring flowers.*

tainly intends for you to become a saint." We should engrave these words of Saint Ignatius of Loyola in our hearts. There is great reason for joy — *even* amidst our trials and sufferings.

Joy is not the absence of suffering: It is the presence of God.

As many of you know, I lost my beloved mother to cancer. When Mom was nearing the end of her life, during her final hours with us, in spite of the unbearable sorrow and heartache I felt at the prospect of losing such a precious mother, I found myself praying with all my heart: "My God, I love You! My God, I love You!" I thought it was mysterious that this was the sentiment pouring from my heart during that time when I was in the depths of crushing sorrow. But that is a sign of the Holy Spirit: when He fills our hearts with love for Him in *spite* of our pain. The Holy Spirit is there to help us through *everything*. God's Spirit is love, and love makes everything easier to endure.

Mom used to tell us: "Remember that the fruit of the Holy Spirit is love, joy, peace, patience, gentleness, long-suffering" and so on. She was always inspiring us to *remember* the fruits of the Holy Spirit. Keep these in your mind and heart — these beautiful fruits.

After Mom gave her spirit back to God, Dad and all ten children gathered around her to cry, pray, and share memories of our life together as a family. Later that morning, as I stood in the corner of the room looking at my sweet mother's body before they took her away, I sensed a *sweetness* in the room — a sweet consolation, a sweet *presence*, in spite of our intense sorrow. That, too, is the Holy Spirit, the Comforter, the Consoler. Right there with us.

More recently, I lost my dad at Christmas time. I had always had my dad by my side throughout all my life. Almost *every* day for four-and-a-half years since losing Mom, Dad and I went to the cemetery together to make a visit and pray at Mom's grave site. Even in the snow, we went to her place of rest to pray. I had the privilege of being my dad's primary caregiver for those final years of his life. It was a very sorrowful winter when he passed away, one of the most sorrowful of my entire life, trying to adjust to life as an orphan. Surprisingly, during this time of intense grief, a friend faraway encouraged me to smile at the children around me, at my nieces and nephews. I found that in doing so, in spite of my own misery, it uplifted and consoled me. If we try to smile and bring joy to others even in the midst of our own sadness, love carries us through.

You might be familiar with the news that came out about Mother Teresa after she was called home to God, the news about her "dark night of the soul," the interior sufferings she underwent during the last fifty years of her life. Jesus had told her ahead of time that she would suffer greatly but not to be afraid because He would be with her through it all. He told her to "smile more tenderly" (in *spite* of her own sufferings) and to go into the dark places and bring Christ's light of love. He wanted her to go into the black holes of Calcutta, to the unhappy homes of the poor and destitute. He said that the poorest of the poor don't love Him because they don't know Him. And He said: **"Come, be my light."** I think that's what Jesus wants *all* of us to do.

Mother Teresa brightened up the whole world for us with her smile, even when she was suffering inside more than any of us knew. That is *our* mission too: to bring the light of Christ to others. To "be the sunshine of God's love" to all we meet, as Mother Teresa would say.

Our Lord Himself told Mother Teresa: "You will suffer much, but I will be with you." He told her to pray more fervently, make more sacrifices, and *"smile more tenderly."*

Saint Thérèse said that we should smile even when we think we are alone, because the angels are watching! Her exact words were: "Even when alone be cheerful, remembering always that you are in the sight of the angels."

If you want to know the best thing you can do for the world, the best thing you can do for our country, and the best thing you can do for your family, it is to become HOLY. As I have grown, I have learned that we can't always change others; we can't always change the behavior of others. We can only change ourselves for the better, and that is challenge enough! Strive to overcome yourself and your own sins and weaknesses with the help of God's grace. Become more virtuous. Start living a more honorable, honest, holy, humble, loving, and faithful life starting today. Begin to smile more because "a smile is the beginning of love," as Mother Teresa used to say. In this way, you will become a light to others — just like the sunlight touching the top of Maine's Mount Katahdin and then spreading across America. And remember that we can't do that — we can't become holy — without *Jesus*. All life and all holiness come from *Him*. That is why coming to Christ is so important.

Always remember, too, that "joy isn't found in the material objects surrounding us — but in the inner recesses of the soul."

*Sun setting over Mount Katahdin and continuing
its course across our country as we filmed
our final episode of* Coming to Christ.

Joy is to be found in Jesus, Who said, "I am always in your heart." Saint Thérèse also said that "one can possess joy in a prison cell as well as in a palace." Riches don't bring happiness. LOVE does. Holiness does. Doing God's will does. "Nothing will afford you more joy and satisfaction than the perfect fulfilling of God's will," as Thomas à Kempis says in *The Imitation of Christ*.

May all of heaven help us to come to Christ and faithfully fulfill our Father's will, thus drawing nearer to the God of our gladness and joy!

In *The Joy of the Gospel*, Pope Francis reminds us: "The joy of the Gospel fills the hearts and lives of all who encounter Jesus. Those who accept His offer of salvation are set free from sin, sorrow, inner emptiness, and loneliness. With Christ, joy is constantly born anew."

And this brings me to one last thought before we conclude this reflection.

I have been reading *The Dialogue of Saint Catherine of Siena*. What is astounding about her is that she was believed to be illiterate — yet she is not only a canonized saint, she is a Doctor of the Church! (I love how in God's family, in the Catholic Church, even if you are completely poor and illiterate, you can become a great saint!) This book was dictated by Saint Catherine during a state of ecstasy while she was in dialogue with God our Father! In His messages to her, God talks about the purpose of our existence — which is God — and He explains how to *reach* Him, which is what this whole presentation is all about!

Here is what our Heavenly Father said to Saint Catherine of Siena: First, He said, "I wish for no other thing than love." We are to be *bound* to God with love. We are made *new* through "the total love of God." He also said: "She renders to me the sweet odor of glory and praise to My Name, and so fulfills the object of her creation. In this way, therefore, she reaches the term of her being, that is Myself, her God, Who am eternal life."

We reach God and eternal life by offering the sweet fragrance of *glory and praise to God's Holy Name* and *thus* we come to reach God and possess God. That is the joy of all joys!!!

Always remember: Possessing God is the joy of all joys!

He is my exceeding joy (cf. Psalm 43:4).

As we prepare to leave this special place where the sunlight touches America first and then spreads across our land, let me share these beautiful words by Pope Emeritus Benedict XVI:

> The happiness you are seeking, the happiness you have a right to enjoy has a name and a face: It is Jesus of Nazareth, hidden in the Eucharist. Only He gives the fullness of life to humanity! (Address to Young People, August 18, 2005)

In closing, I want to share a prayer that I learned from Mother Teresa with some of her secrets of finding joy:

> Immaculate Heart of Mary, cause of our joy, pray for us, bless us, keep us in your most pure heart, help us to do all the good we can, so that we may please Jesus — through you, with you, and in you. Immaculate Heart of Mary, cause of our joy, pray for us!

ɷ

Thank you for sharing in these reflections on coming to Christ. May we follow His divine light, with the help of His grace, and greet each other in heaven.

A beautiful sunrise on Willard Beach.

ACKNOWLEDGMENTS

My most heartfelt gratitude goes above all to Our Heavenly Father for the priceless gift of His only-begotten Son and the equally precious gift of faith that enables us to *come* to Christ and attain everlasting life "through Him, with Him, and in Him." I lovingly thank Our Blessed Mother Mary, too, for giving us Our Savior.

This naturally leads to acknowledging my own dear parents, Francis and Ruth Conroy, who taught me everything I know about coming to Christ. Without this treasure of faith that they handed on to us with such great love and care, the first gift of life would have been a fatal one. Thank you, Mom and Dad, with all my heart and soul — and then some! I love you from here to Eternity.

This book blossomed from a television series on EWTN. With great joy and affection, I want to thank the EWTN executives, Doug Keck and Peter Gagnon, who took a gigantic leap of faith in sending a camera crew to Maine to film these presentations *outdoors*. Each additional member of the team likewise deserves special recognition for what they accomplished: John Kuklinski, Jr., Mark Kaczperski, Michael Celeri, and Bob Blake. With the less than favorable weather conditions during the time of their visit, it appeared that the whole venture might be a washout! Thank you, Doug and Peter, and all of the crew, for believing that we could do it. Thank you for your heroic efforts to share God's glorious creation with all of our EWTN viewers, and now with our readers. Your courageous faith is *inspiring* to me!

I am deeply touched by the kindness and giftedness of our photographer, Lisa, of Lisa Elizabeth Photography in Falmouth, Maine. She took most of the pictures throughout this book, and she went well beyond her call of duty by providing water to the film crew, as well as a warm blanket and fleece jacket for my shoulders and legs during the more chilly shoots along the ocean. How thoughtful she was to us all. Lisa, you are a gem! We all appreciate you so much.

I also want to thank Peter Gagnon, John Kuklinski, Jr., Mary Beth Parent, Shirley Estabrooks, and Denise Boutin for contributing photographs to this project. As Mother Teresa used to say, "Alone we can do nothing, but together we can do something beautiful for God."

I am grateful to all of the wonderful people who allowed us to film at these particular locations in the state of Maine, including Robert Malley at Portland Head Light, Lorenzo at the Lobster Shack, and Carolyn and Bob Gilman at their log cabin in Benedicta, along with their beloved son and daughter-in-law Robb and Rachel Gilman. I honestly can't thank you enough! We couldn't have done this without you.

I am deeply touched by Mike and Antoinette Meehan, who helped me to care for the EWTN crew during their stay. And I want to thank Pat Smith of Ohio for inviting me to prepare the spiritual talks that ultimately developed into this new television series and book.

I owe a special debt of gratitude to the beautiful Magnificat Ladies prayer group in Maine, under the patronage of "Our Lady, Queen of Humility." As soon as they discovered that four members of the camera crew from EWTN had never been to Maine before, and realizing that I would be tied up during the course of these tapings, the Magnificat Ladies helped me to feed them! They graciously prepared a beautiful home-cooked meal for the crew as a warm welcome on the first night of their visit and provided gift bags full of delicious treats. They even made a "Welcome to Maine, EWTN" sign! Most beautiful and meaningful of all, they "stormed the gates of heaven" with their prayers for the success of these tapings, helping us to pull it off between the raindrops, just in the nick of time! Cindi Schaab, Cindy Andreson, Carolyn Gilman, Nancy Hall, Cathy Koenig, and all the Magnificat Ladies of prayer — I thank you and I love you!

୭

owner. (Any emphasis in these texts has been added by the author.)

Quotations from papal statements and documents and other Vatican documents are copyrighted, © 2014, Libreria Editrice Vaticana.

Diary of St. Maria Faustina Kowalska: Divine Mercy in My Soul © 1987 Marian Fathers of the Immaculate Conception of the B.V.M. All rights reserved. Used with permission. (Cited as "*Diary.*")

PHOTO CREDITS

Page 5: Susan Conroy.

Page 6: Susan Conroy.

Page 8: Lisa Elizabeth Photography, Falmouth, Maine.

Page 12: Lisa Elizabeth Photography, Falmouth, Maine.

Page 15: Lisa Elizabeth Photography, Falmouth, Maine.

Page 17: Susan Conroy.

Page 20: Susan Conroy.

Page 24: John Dana © 2012.

Page 37: Susan Conroy.

Page 38: Lisa Elizabeth Photography, Falmouth, Maine.

Page 43: Susan Conroy.

Page 45: Shirley Estabrooks.

Page 48: Shirley Estabrooks.

Page 55 (top): Susan Conroy; *(bottom)* Susan Conroy.

Page 58: Lisa Elizabeth Photography, Falmouth, Maine.

Page 61: Susan Conroy.

Page 68: Susan Conroy.

Page 76: Susan Conroy.

Page 78: Peter Gagnon.

Page 80: Mary Beth Parent.

Page 86: Mary Beth Parent.

Page 87: Mary Beth Parent.

Page 95: Susan Conroy.

Page 97: Mary Beth Parent.

Page 98: Mary Beth Parent.

Page 103: Mary Beth Parent.
Page 108 (top): Denise Boutin; *(bottom)* Susan Conroy.
Page 111: Mary Beth Parent.
Page 115: John Kuklinski, Jr.
Page 119: Susan Conroy.